Infinite Upgrades

Need It? Want It? Short on Cash or Credit?
Get to Your YES Today!

Marian Snow

Ethan Madison
PUBLISHING

Privacy and Illustrative Use Notice: Certain names, identifying details, and circumstances have been changed to protect the privacy of individuals referenced in this work. Some stories are composites drawn from multiple real experiences and are intended to illustrate broader themes and situations.

References to companies, products, services, organizations, and brands are provided for educational, informational, and illustrative purposes only and should not be interpreted as endorsements, sponsorships, or formal affiliations unless expressly stated.

ISBN: 978-0-9790142-8-4

Published by Ethan Madison Publishing, Chicago IL

First Edition: March 2026

Printed in the United States of America

Disclaimer: This book is for informational purposes only and is not intended as financial, investment, tax, or legal advice. Consult with qualified professionals before making any decisions. The author and publisher disclaim any liability for losses incurred as a result of following the information in this book.

Formatted with Vellum

Also by Marian Snow

Stop Sitting on Your Assets

#1 Amazon Bestseller

Real Estate & Retirement Planning

* * *

Transparency Note from the Author

At the time of writing this book, I do not receive compensation from any of the companies, brands, or services referenced in these pages. No affiliate links. No sponsorships. No kickbacks.

This book reflects my own observations, research, experiences, and interpretation of broader social and economic trends. Any references to companies, products, services, organizations, or brands are for informational and illustrative purposes only and should not be interpreted as endorsements, sponsorships, or formal affiliations.

The companies referenced help illustrate a shift I believe is reshaping how millions of Americans think about ownership, access, flexibility, and the navigation of everyday life.

Names have been changed to protect privacy. Some examples and stories are composites created from multiple real-world experiences.

My goal is simple: to explore an idea I find fascinating and increasingly important — and to invite you to think about it for yourself.

* * *

Contents

Foreword

Something remarkable has quietly transformed American consumer life. Millions of people have canceled cable for Netflix, ditched CDs for Spotify, summoned an Uber instead of financing a second car, and booked an Airbnb rather than buying a vacation home.

They lease instead of buy. They subscribe instead of purchase. They flex instead of commit. And they do it intelligently, confidently, and without apology. Nobody questioned the choice. It simply made sense. We called it smart.

That same intelligence has now arrived at your door. *Infinite Upgrades* applies this wisdom beyond streaming and ride-sharing to the furniture in your living room, the appliances in your kitchen, the tires on your car, and the technology in your hands. It's not a lesser way to live, nor necessarily a compromise. For many people, it can be a better path that begins with one better question: "Can I afford to own it?" or "Does owning it actually make my life better?" Those are different questions, and they open the door to much better answers.

You are no longer limited to buying outright with cash, credit, or a charge card. That is simply not the only way to access the things that:

- improve your home surroundings
- make you safer on the road
- get you a better night's sleep
- keep you connected and informed
- entertain you for a laugh after a long day
- get you where you need to go
- bring your family together at the table
- make your chores easier
- outfit your wardrobe or your home

The list is endless.

And when it fits your life and feels right for you, simply choosing access may very well be the wisest choice available.

The time for this fresh perspective is not coming.

It is here.

Welcome to *Infinite Upgrades: Need It? Want It? Short on Cash or Credit? Get to Your YES Today*! A new way of thinking about what it means to live abundantly, intentionally, and entirely on your own terms.

* * *

Introduction

This book has one simple goal: to help you think differently about the stuff in your life.

The couch you sink into after a long day.

The fridge that keeps your food fresh.

The tires that get you where you need to go.

The technology you use every day.

There's a possibly smarter, more freeing, and more flexible way to have these things. A way that breaks the old rules most of us grew up believing.

You don't need a finance degree to understand it. You don't need perfect credit, a fat savings account, or a spreadsheet open on your laptop. What you need is a little curiosity and the willingness to consider that the ways you were taught may not be the only way. Or even the best way.

Because here's something you may find yourself recognizing right away. You've probably already been simply choosing access without even realizing it.

If you've ever rented a musical instrument for your child's school band, leased a car instead of buying one, streamed shows on Netflix instead of owning DVDs, or brought something home on payments and returned it when life changed, then you have already been on this very path.

You've been living it. You just may not have had a name for it.

Who Moved the Goalpost?

For generations the dream was pretty straightforward: work, save, buy, own. Ownership was the finish line. The beacon on the hill. The proof you had made it.

Your grandfather's 1955 washing machine lasted thirty years.

Today, we all face a world of lightning-speed innovation, where your new purchase can become outdated in almost the blink of an eye. Our grandparents never had to worry whether the phone on the wall would become obsolete. In our modern world it's expected.

Rent-to-own showed up in the beginning as a practical bridge to help families reach the goal of ownership. It originally let you bring something useful home while you worked toward owning it outright. The name itself, "rent-to-own," made the destination clear.

Then the goalpost moved.

For the first group, it moved because the old finish line had simply gotten too far away. Home prices soared, credit tightened, and traditional paths to ownership became out of reach for many good, responsible families.

For the second, the destination itself changed. They looked at ownership, really looked at it, and decided that the weight of maintenance, repairs, storage, and eventual selling no longer served the life they actually wanted to live.

And for the third fastest-growing group, the goalpost moved because the world now moves too quickly for ownership to even make sense.

Three different reasons. Three different kinds of people. And one silent, practical, deeply human solution that turns out to be perfectly designed for all three.

This shift isn't happening in isolation. Consumers have already shown a growing willingness to choose access over ownership in category after category.

Streaming replaced DVD collections. Software became subscriptions. Transportation became increasingly on-demand. Across much of modern life, people are choosing flexibility, convenience, and relevance over permanent possession. This shift has increasingly expanded opportunities for access-based models in countless categories.

In his book *Purple Cow*, Seth Godin reminds us that in a world full of average, the only way to stand out is to be remarkable, and remarkable often means being flexible. He argues that the smartest offerings are the ones that serve people right where they are, in this moment of their lives, without locking them into something that will soon feel heavy or outdated.

Strategist Robbie Kellman Baxter captured the same shift in *The Membership Economy*, describing a massive transformation happening in everyday life: a move from ownership to access, from one-time transactions to ongoing relationships. As she states it so simply, “It’s not about ownership; it’s about access, options, and freedom.”

That same spirit lives at the heart of choosing access: it keeps options open, lets families stay light, and frees them to pivot gracefully whenever life asks them to.

That idea sits at the heart of what so many Americans are discovering today. Choosing access lets you enjoy what serves you right now: whether it’s a reliable refrigerator, safe tires, or a high-definition TV, without getting stuck owning something, dealing with surprise repair bills, or hanging onto it when you discover you no longer need it six months, or even a couple years, from now.

Instead, today's smartest folks value flexibility and keeping things relevant more than being stuck with long-term commitments.

That's exactly what choosing access (like through rent-to-own, lease-to-own or similar models) brings to the table. It keeps your options open, helps your family stay in sync with whatever life is asking for right now, and lets you adapt gracefully, without any guilt or heavy anchors holding you back.

Rent-to-own was built to help people reach the same goals that prior generations had sought. As it turns out, it may be even better suited for a world where that finish line has dissolved away, where the destination is no longer a paid-in-full receipt in a drawer, but a life that fits who you really are, right now, with the freedom to change course whenever life asks you to.

That's what this book is about.

Not just the "rent" or "lease" part. And not just the "own" part.

The flexible space in between, where real life happens.

The Simple Argument

Here's the one idea I hope sticks with you: For a growing number of us, for reasons that are practical, financial, and deeply personal, choosing access over ownership isn't settling for less. It's choosing wisely.

One thing worth saying clearly, right up front: if you have the cash or qualifying credit to buy something outright at a reasonable rate, that will almost always be the cheaper path on paper. This book does not pretend otherwise.

What it argues, and what the evidence supports, is that for a growing number of Americans, those options simply aren't available at the moment they're needed. And that even for those who do have options, the value of flexibility, freedom from maintenance, and the ability to walk away can be worth more than the price difference. The math depends entirely on your circumstances. What this book will do is make sure you understand the options you truly have.

One more thing worth saying upfront: This approach works best when you use it with intention. Access what you need. Return what doesn't serve you anymore. And every so often, take stock. That subscription you signed up for last year and haven't touched in months? That's just clutter in a different form. We'll talk more about that later.

What This Book Actually Is

Infinite Upgrades is a celebration of a smarter, lighter way to live. It's the story of a model that has been steadily serving everyday real Americans for over a century. From the Singer sewing machine to the smartphone, from the parlor piano to the prescription mobility scooter. And today, it's more regulated, more transparent, and more genuinely built for real families than ever before.

This is not an advertisement for particular companies. The rent-to-own world has good operators and not-so-good ones, just like every other industry. Smart shoppers always ask good questions, and this book will help you ask the right ones.

Above all, this is an invitation.

An invitation to look clearly at a financial tool that has been hidden behind outdated assumptions, and finally see it for what it really is.

How to Read This Book

You don't have to read it cover to cover.

If you are the kind of reader who loves the full story. The history, the philosophy, the human stakes, the financial argument. It is all here, and it builds deliberately from page one.

But if you're a dipper or a skimmer (and most of us are), this book is built for you too. Each chapter stands on its own. Jump to the stories in Chapters 4 and 7 if you want to meet some of the real families first. There are many others sprinkled throughout. Jump to Chapter 18 if you want the practical "Let's Make It Work for You" guide right away. Or flip to the state-by-state guide in the back if you want to know your rights before you read another word.

This book was written for the way people read in the real world. From those who are deliberate and steady, to those with a short attention-span or only have moments to spare in their busy lives.

What You Will Find Inside

We start where the story actually begins. Not in a corporate boardroom or a policy brief, but in a family home, in a human need, in the oldest and most honest of questions: how do I get what my family needs without waiting. And with the resources I have right now?

From there, we move through the full landscape of what access looks like in modern American life. From furniture and appliances to electronics, tires, mobility devices, and even HVAC and storage buildings. You will meet real people whose lives were changed not by luck or windfall, but by workable, dignified solutions that met them where they were.

You will find the financial argument, the truthful one, the one that compares the real cost of ownership against the true value of the option to keep or return an item. You may find the math more interesting than conventional wisdom ever acknowledged.

You will find the regulatory story, forty-seven states, the FTC, and four decades of consumer advocacy. These elements are important, because informed readers make better decisions and deserve to know that this model has been rigorously accountable for a long time.

And you will find the tools to use it wisely if it fits your life. Not because you have to, but because you choose to.

Is This Book For You?

There are a few important "ifs" that could make this story feel like it's written just for you, and for so many people you see everywhere in your daily life.

United Way researchers who studied how normal folks in America really experience their lives gave a name to the largest group among them. These are the ones who earn a paycheck, pay their taxes, and keep their communities running, yet live one unexpected bill away from a crisis. They call them

ALICE: Asset Limited, Income Constrained, Employed. If that description feels familiar, if you have been there, are there now, or know and love someone who is, this book was written with you at the center of every page.

If you have ever felt the deep frustration of needing something your budget couldn't absorb all at once, this book is for you.

If you have ever moved to a new city, started over after a hard season, or found yourself furnishing a life from scratch with limited resources, this book is for you.

If you are a parent trying to provide for your family without sacrificing your financial future, this book is for you.

If you are simply curious about a smarter, lighter way to live, this book is especially for you.

Forget the need to know every detail before you take a single step. You can walk away from a rent-to-own, lease-to-own or rental-purchase agreement at just about any time. The exit door is always open. You are never locked in beyond your next payment. That is not a loophole. That is the entire design.

This isn't meant to be the final word on every financial decision you'll ever make. It's meant to make sure you know your options and that you feel equipped to direct your own life.

Clearing Up the Language

Throughout the book you'll see "rent-to-own"(RTO) and "lease-to-own" (LTO) used interchangeably. You will also see the terms: "rental-purchase" and "lease-purchase." These all describe the exact same thing.

All reference a lease or rental transaction, and not a credit-based loan. No debt. No interest. No long-term obligation. You can stop anytime.

That distinction matters. "Lease" can sound corporate. "Rent" can sound temporary. Neither word fully captures the dignity and amount of choice you retain. But by the time you finish this book, I hope no term referenced carries any shadow at all.

Merriam-Webster defines *possession* this way: 'control [ ] of property without regard to ownership.' That is exactly what a lease-to-own agreement delivers from the moment the product comes through your door. You possess it completely. You control it entirely. Ownership, if you choose it, follows later. But the life you are living with it begins on day one.

One last clarification: This model works best with durable goods. Things that can be taken home, used, returned if needed, maintained, and re-leased to someone else. Refrigerators, sofas, tires, laptops, gaming systems, sheds and more. These are the kinds of products the system was built for.

A Note on the People in These Pages

You'll meet real people in this book. Some are composites drawn from many true experiences, others are real individuals who generously shared their stories. Names and identifying details have been changed to protect privacy.

They are not extraordinary. That's the point.

They are the family on the block, the single mom in the apartment upstairs, the new arrival building a life from scratch, the retiree navigating a changing world with dignity and grace. Every day Americans making clear-eyed, practical, forward-looking decisions about how to furnish their lives.

These folks are just a small sampling of the millions who are already choosing access and living lighter.

Not because they had to.

Because they understood that they could.

* * *

Chapter 1

It Was Always This Way

If you think that choosing access over ownership is some shiny new idea cooked up by Silicon Valley. It isn't.

Long before Netflix, Spotify, or Uber ever existed, you and millions of other American families were already solving the same common problem the same practical way: "I need this right now, but I don't have the full amount today. So how do I make it happen?"

The question wasn't theoretical. It was practical. You simply got creative.

You brought things home first. You paid over time. And then decided, along the way, whether those things had earned a permanent place in your life.

From Singer to Piano Keys

In the mid-1800s, a sewing machine wasn't a luxury. It was a lifeline. It meant clothes for the family, extra income for the household, and real independence for the woman operating it. It meant independence for households that had very few paths to it.

But there was a problem. Most families couldn't afford one outright.

Isaac Merritt Singer understood that hunger. When his company started letting families take a sewing machine home and pay for it over time, something important shifted. Ownership was no longer an all-or-nothing leap. It became something you could grow into.

Use it first. Pay a little at a time. Own it when you're ready.

It was a simple shift, but it changed the nature of the decision. Families no longer had to be certain on day one. They could live with the machine, benefit from it, and grow into ownership over time. What mattered wasn't whether they could afford it all at once. It was whether it made sense in their lives.

Once that door opened, it remained forever that way.

The same pattern showed up in a different part of the home.

The piano.

For many families, the piano wasn't just an instrument. It was something more—a symbol of progress, of culture, of a life that felt a little more complete. But like the sewing machine, it came with a price that most families couldn't meet upfront.

So they thought them out of reach.

Then families were offered the opportunity to bring home pianos from companies like Baldwin. Not in one big purchase, but week by week, month by month.

The piano became the heart of the home. It emerged as a place for music, laughter, and family pride. It wasn't about instant ownership. It was about access first, ownership later.

By the early 1900s, the phonograph had followed. The Victrola, which later became a part of RCA, brought recorded music into the home for the first time. Families who had never heard a symphony orchestra could now hear one without leaving their parlors.

It was access first, ownership later.

Then came the radio. RCA and Zenith placed receivers into homes across the country so families could gather in the evenings to be entertained and hear of world events.

Next was television. Brands like Curtis Mathes let people bring those big sets home using rent-to-own plans. When Curtis Mathes later launched *ColorTyme* to offer color TVs the same way, they weren't inventing anything new. They were simply continuing a tradition that was already well established.

And for generations, the telephone itself wasn't owned at all. It was rented from AT&T. The most essential communication device in American life, the tool that connected every home to every other, was accessed, not purchased. Nobody thought twice about it.

The Chill That Delivered Miracles

It is difficult to think of another household invention that so overwhelmingly transformed everyday life than the refrigerator. When the first electric refrigerators appeared in America, they were nothing short of miraculous. They kept food cold without ice, the required daily delivery service to keep it, and the constant worry that tomorrow's dinner would spoil overnight.

There was only one problem. In 1923, one of the first successful mass-produced electric refrigerators, Kelvinator, sold for **$525**. A brand-new Ford 2-seater Model-T was selling for **$269**. Think about that for a moment. A refrigerator would have cost a family more than double the sticker price of a new car.

Over a century later, that $525 price tag would translate to $10,250 in today's economy.

Every family wanted what the refrigerator promised: safer food, less waste, fewer trips to the market, and the confidence that tomorrow's dinner would still be waiting. What stood in the way wasn't desire. It was the fact that almost no working household could afford one.

Families needed a different way to access those life-changing and time-saving benefits. Enter hire-purchase. Pay a little now. Pay a little next month. Take the refrigerator home today.

That simple idea unlocked millions of kitchen doors.

Engineers had invented the wonder-machine that preserved food, yet it did not transform America the day it was invented. It actually transformed America the day average families could afford to bring one home.

The Idea That Traveled

This wasn't just an American story. The same instinct appeared in Europe as "hire purchase" as well. It adapted through every wave of progress - electrification, new appliances, faster innovation.

Each time the world moved forward, the question was always the same: How can regular people get this now, not someday?

The answer kept coming back the same way: Take it home. Use it. Let the rest unfold over time.

By the middle of the 20th century, this approach felt completely normal. Living rooms were furnished, kitchens became equipped, and homes slowly transformed. Not through one massive purchase, but through steady, manageable steps.

What looked like a financial arrangement was really something more human: a bridge between what you dreamed of and what you could handle today.

From Silent Screen to the Stream

It started in darkened rooms, almost by accident, flickering black and white images on a wall while a piano player in the corner did his best to enhance your experience. No sound from the screen. Just pictures, movement, and imagination filling in the rest. People thought it was magic. They paid a nickel to sit in the dark and watch it.

Then came the talkies. Then color. Then the great movie palaces, which were ornate theaters with velvet seats and chandeliers. A place where going to the pictures was an event, a destination, an occasion to dress-up for. For decades, if you wanted to see a movie, you went where the movie was.

Then something shifted.

A company called Blockbuster learned that people really wanted the movies to come to them. They stocked thousands of VHS and beta videotapes and opened stores in every neighborhood in America. And here's the detail most people have forgotten: in the early days, not everyone owned a VCR. So, Blockbuster rented those, as well. You rented the machine to watch the movie you rented.

Access layered on access. The same instinct that Singer had with the sewing machine, a hundred years later, appeared in those strip malls.

Then DVDs replaced tapes. Blockbuster adapted briefly. Then a company called Netflix mailed you the disc directly to your home in an iconic red envelope. You kept it as long as you wanted and dropped it back in the mailbox when you were done. No late fees. No driving. Access, delivered.

But even that wasn't convenient enough.

Along came Redbox, with its bright red vending machine the size of a refrigerator, planted right where you already shopped. Grocery stores.

Walgreens. Walmart. A dollar a night, no membership, no clerk, no conversation required. You grabbed your movie on the way home and dropped it back the next morning. By 2007 Redbox had more locations across America than Blockbuster. The vending machine beat the store.

Then the disc disappeared entirely.

Today Netflix streams thousands of films and shows directly to any screen in your home, instantly, for a flat monthly fee. No disc to store. No envelope to mail back. No machine to return it to. You don't want a physical object at all. You just want to be entertained. And now you can be, anywhere, anytime, without owning a single frame of it.

That journey, from the nickel theater to the streaming service, took about a century. And every step of the way, the direction of travel was the same: from ownership toward access. From going where the thing was to having it come to you. From buying the object to buying the experience.

Movies didn't get worse. They got better. And the way people access them got simpler and more flexible with every generation.

Not just movies. Not just streaming. But every category of life where the same evolution is silently, steadily underway. Where the question has shifted from, "Do I own it?" to, "Do I have it when I need it?"

The Man Who Had an Epiphany

It is in Dr. Charles Smitherman's landmark book, *The Rent-to-Own Revolution: The Definitive Industry History of Advocacy and Consumer Access*, that one of the most important origin stories in the industry's history is told with the depth it deserves. The rent-to-own business has no single founder — it grew from conditions, not from one person's blueprint. But it does have a moment everything changed. And Dr. Smitherman pinpointed that event to have sparked in Wichita, Kansas.

In the early 1960s, an appliance dealer named Ernie Talley was watching the same pattern repeat itself in his store. Families came in wanting refrigerators, washers, televisions. They were denied credit or they feared the harsh terms of installment contracts. Some tried renting as a stopgap, by paying week to week with no clear path to owning. Over time, Talley noticed something that troubled him: many of these families were paying more in total rent than the product's actual retail value, yet still had nothing to show for it.

That realization changed everything.

He didn't ask, 'How much more can I collect?' He asked something far more important: 'What is actually fair here?' His answer was simple and radical for its time: when a customer had effectively paid the value of a product through their rental payments, he considered it theirs. No more collecting. No legal leverage over a family who had already paid what the thing was worth.

By 1963, that simple sense of fairness had become a formal business, Mr. T's Rental. It was straightforward: families could take home appliances or furniture immediately, pay in small weekly or monthly increments, and return the product if necessary. No credit needed. No long-term obligation. If the household kept paying long enough, title transferred. Naturally, with no drama.

Mr. T's grew into a regional chain across Kansas, Missouri, and Oklahoma. Other entrepreneurs watched, recognized the same unmet need in their own communities, and built their own versions. The transaction was simple. The barrier to entry was low. And the need for immediate access to essential goods without the risk of punishing debt already existed everywhere.

That intuition became an industry. And the industry, at its best, has never entirely lost sight of it.

And so what would become rent-to-own wasn't cooked up by a corporate think-tank. It grew organically from a moral intuition about how ordinary people deserve to be treated, and from a practical recognition that need doesn'tt wait for perfect financial conditions.

The idea had been traveling for a century before Ernie Talley gave it its modern form. Singer had carried it. Baldwin had carried it. The Victrola, the radio, the telephone, all of them had carried it. Talley simply saw it clearly, named it honorably, and built something around it that has never stopped growing.

That is the foundation on which everything in this book rests.

Ernie Talley may not have used these exact words, but what he built carried *Four Core Truths* that still define the best of rent-to-own today. These truths were later clearly documented and championed by the Association of Professional Rental Organizations, known as APRO, the national trade association that has represented the industry since 1980. Here they are in plain language:

- RTO is a lease, not a loan. No debt, no interest, no long-term obligation. You can return the item anytime and walk away clean.
- RTO is flexible. You stay in control. Keep paying toward ownership, buy it out early when it makes sense, or return it if your life shifts.
- RTO comes with service and maintenance. When something breaks, someone handles the fix. No surprise repair bills.

- RTO is regulated and transparent. 47 states have specific laws governing these agreements, with clear disclosures and real consumer protections. Federal FTC oversight applies as well.

These aren't abstract rules. You see them in real life. You see them in the single mom who finally gets a reliable refrigerator, in the veteran who brings home a couch after deployment, in the family that keeps moving forward even when money gets tight

Forged Over A Century

When you explore rent-to-own or lease-to-own today, you're not stepping into something experimental or unproven. You're connecting with a forged idea that has been stress-tested for more than a century.

The names of the products have changed. Today it may be a sofa, a laptop, a refrigerator, or a set of tires. But the underlying truth remains remarkably consistent: people have always found ways to align what they need with what they can manage. Not all at once, but in time.

More Americans are finding that access is the answer, and they're finding it available in more and more areas of life. The tool that's been providing that answer for over a century is what this book is here to explore.

Access isn't the exception.

It's pretty much the rule that was always there.

* * *

Chapter 2

You Were Already
Ahead of the Curve

Meet Maya

Maya was thirty two and had built a life that would have confused her parents.

She worked remotely three days a week from a small apartment that always looked cleaner on Zoom than it did in real life. Two unpacked moving boxes still sat in the corner of her bedroom nearly a year after she moved in. At this point they had become furniture.

Her monthly expenses looked less like ownership and more like a collection of tiny permissions. Spotify. Netflix. Adobe. Cloud storage. A meditation app she forgot to cancel twice. A meal kit subscription she swore she would start using again next month. Rides through Lyft when parking downtown sounded exhausting. Grocery delivery during busy weeks. DoorDash more often than she admitted to herself.

Her friends teased her because she subscribed to everything except downtime.

She owned some things, of course. A laptop covered in coffee stickers. A couch that barely fit through the doorway when it was delivered. A houseplant leaning dramatically toward the only window with decent light, surviving mostly through stubbornness and irregular watering.

What she didn't have were shelves lined with DVDs or closets packed with things she rarely touched. Most of what remained from earlier versions of her life lived in a few dusty boxes tucked into the corner of her parents' garage, where childhood keepsakes, old textbooks, and half-forgotten college memories had survived three moves and at least two promises to finally sort through them.

That said, her current place was light, flexible, and temporary by design. She liked knowing that if a better job appeared in another city, or if she decided six months from now that she wanted a different neighborhood, most of her life could be packed into a moving truck over a weekend.

To Maya, access didn't feel like sacrifice, but instead felt like breathing room.

She wasn't missing anything. She was free.

Then There's Max

Max could be difficult to pin down.

At thirty five, he had already lived in four cities, changed careers twice, and could tell you the fastest route through three major airports but still needed GPS to find the storage unit where half the possessions he still hangs onto now live. His work shifted constantly. Some months he was traveling three weeks out of four. Other months he worked remotely from coffee shops, airports, or the small rental house he barely occupied enough to justify paying for.

His calendar looked like someone had spilled appointments across it.

He forgot birthdays. Missed emails. Accidentally paid for two music streaming services for almost a year before noticing.

Friends joked that Max subscribed to things faster than he canceled them.

And honestly, they were right.

But Max had also learned something important. Very little in his life stayed still for long.

A new opportunity could appear on Tuesday and have him boarding a plane Thursday morning. A project could end suddenly. A better one could replace it a month later. Cities changed. Relationships changed. Priorities changed.

So he stopped organizing his life around permanence.

His car? Accessed when he needed reliability without long commitments. Entertainment? Subscriptions. Software? Monthly plans. Transportation? Whatever got him where he needed to be fastest. Furniture? Enough to make a place comfortable without turning moving day into a logistical crisis.

He still owned things. Too many charging cables. Hiking gear he swore he would use more often. Boxes from earlier versions of his life stacked in that distant storage unit.

But ownership was no longer the organizing principle of his life.

Motion was.

To Max, flexibility wasn't a philosophy. It was survival.

Stories like Maya's and Max's demonstrate exactly what author Seth Godin means when he talks about serving people right where they are. They choose access that stays personally relevant and flexible instead of locking themselves into ownership that might not fit six months from now. They grant permission on their own terms and can walk away cleanly when life shifts, with no guilt and no heavy anchors.

Max would be the first to tell you his choices aren't right for everyone. Some people crave the deep roots of ownership, the pride of saying "This is mine." But he stands as living proof of something powerful: choosing access isn't a consolation prize for those who can't afford to own. It's a deliberate, intelligent decision made by people who have thought deeply about what they truly want — and discovered that freedom often feels lighter, sweeter, and more aligned with the life they're building.

I've mentioned Seth Godin earlier, but stories like Maya's and Max's are reflected in what he discussed decades ago in another of his books *Permission Marketing*. He said the strongest relationships are built on permission that can be granted and withdrawn. Lease-to-own works the same way. You give permission to use something for as long as it serves you, with the freedom to stop at any time, without penalty or guilt.

What the Business World Rarely Admits

Maya and Max didn't invent this way of living. They simply discovered, in polished, modern packaging, what millions of common American families had already been practicing for decades, and doing so consistently, practically, and with remarkable resilience.

Think of the *ALICE* households that we met in the Introduction. The nurses pulling down double shifts, the teachers grading papers late into the night, the retail workers and delivery drivers who keep our communities running. They're not "poor" in the traditional sense; they're punching the clock every day, yet one unexpected bill, a broken refrigerator, a car repair, or a child needing a laptop for school, can throw everything off balance.

For them, lease-to-own has never been about luxury or trendiness. It's been about survival with dignity. The family that accessed a refrigerator because going without one wasn't an option for keeping food safe for their kids. The parent who brought home a laptop on flexible payments because their teenager needed it for school today, not after months of saving that might never materialize. The couple who accessed reliable tires because safe transportation to work couldn't wait.

These were all grounded, heartfelt choices made in living rooms and kitchens across the country, long before Netflix turned streaming into a lifestyle, long before Spotify made music feel infinite, long before anyone coined the phrase "subscription economy" in a business school lecture hall.

According to the *2025 Rent-to-Own Industry Health Survey* published by the Association of Professional Rental Organizations (APRO), the rent-to-own industry generates approximately $11.5 billion in annual U.S. revenue and operates through 5,798 storefront locations nationwide. It serves more than 4.6 million American households each year, roughly one in every twenty nine households, with nearly 3 million active customers at any given moment. The industry supports more than 42,000 American jobs and invests nearly $2 billion annually in inventory to keep essential goods available when customers need them.

These aren't the numbers of a niche workaround or a last-resort option. These are the numbers of a mainstream institution that has been showing up for everyday families for generations, while much of the corporate world was still catching up to the idea that flexibility and access could be empowering.

Independent research supports this picture. The Federal Trade Commission, not an industry body, but the federal agency charged with protecting consumers, conducted its own survey of nearly 3,000 RTO/LTO customers and found that the overwhelming majority reported satisfaction with their agreements and said they would use the model again. The same survey found that 68 percent of these customers lived in rural areas or small towns, communities where traditional financing options are often thin or nonexistent.

This wasn't a study commissioned by the industry. It was the government doing its job. And what it found was a model that, in the hands of responsible operators, was genuinely serving the people it was designed to serve.

Troy Knew the Truth in His Bones

After multiple back-to-back deployments overseas, Troy stepped off the plane carrying little more than his duffel bag and the silent weight of his experiences while away.

He had to let that go now. He was home. Images of all the precious moments he had only been able to see through text messages now filled his head.

Far too long.
I've been away from my family for far too long.

After the painful hole that separation had carved between himself and those he loved, one truth kept echoing: he was ready for stability. He needed something solid now.

He was surprised at how quickly he was able to find a small mobile home that seemed like it could be just the right size for all of them, except for one glaring problem. It echoed with emptiness. This sparked more worries:

No money saved up. No credit score after so may years away.

The questions rolled through his head.

OK. So, where do we stand?
What's the plan now?

Still, he thought he knew exactly what he needed to start healing that nagging void he was feeling. Troy had always secretly pictured himself as somewhat of a home chef. He needed the true warm feeling of home now. A refrigerator with lots of space. A stove he could do some serious cooking on, alongside his wife in the role of sous chef. He wanted to look his wife and kids in the eyes, and share laughter over a dinner they had prepared together. A full kitchen that didn't feel temporary and allowed for more than microwave dinners.

Rent-to-own gave him that. He quickly found that the folks there understood his situation, helped him with all the basics and gave him payments he could manage week by week. For the first time in years, he could buy groceries that would stay fresh and cook real, healthy meals. He could sit at the table with his family, the sound of their chatter bouncing off walls that finally felt like theirs, while the aroma of fresh biscuits baking filled their home.

Then life tested him again. A letter arrived telling him that his post-deployment benefits were going to be delayed, with no timeline given for how long. He was counting on that money to supplement his new job.

So, with the same steady resolve that had carried him through deployment, Troy called the store, explained the situation, and returned those beloved appliances. He hated doing it. It felt like watching his hard-won sense of home slip away. Fortunately, out in his shed, he had kept the old tiny refrigerator that didn't chill well and the scratched-up stove with one eye that worked and guessed they would have to make do with those for a bit longer.

To his surprise, the store met him with kindness and clarity. They walked him through what they called the 'reinstatement process' — no shame, no lectures, just practical steps and a reminder that the door was still open. He would have a chance to get his agreement back on track later.

A month or so went by, and when his benefits finally cleared, Troy went back to the RTO store. They reinstated his rental-purchase agreement on the same terms. He walked out with a scheduled appliance delivery once more, continuing straight toward ownership without losing the ground he had already gained. They started cooking their family meals again. And in the peaceful evenings, Troy would sit and feel the deep relief of a plan that had come together. His prized kitchen essentials had waited for him.

That is the calm power of this model. It doesn't demand perfection. It offers understanding.

The Double Standard

Here is something worth noting.

When a young professional like Maya accesses software, streaming, and fitness on flexible terms, we call her savvy and modern. When a mother juggling work and kids, or a veteran like Troy, does something similar with essential household goods, too many voices quickly question their judgment.

This book exists to correct that mistaken double standard.

Because, as we have said, the access revolution didn't start through Silicon Valley design. It started in the kitchens and homes of hard-working families, and in the hearts of people like Troy, who figured out, through necessity and creativity, that ownership isn't the only path to a good life. Sometimes the wisest move is the one that gives you breathing room, workability, and the chance to keep moving forward even when life tries to slow you down.

Chapter 3

Access Everything That Matters

There's a simple human act most everyone does, yet nobody can quite agree on what to call it.

Ask Joanna Gaines, of Fixer-Upper fame, and she'll tell you to *furnish your nest.*

Marie Kondo, the organizing consultant, would gently insist that you *surround yourself only with what sparks joy.*

Oprah might say *create the space where your life can happen.*

Marie Calloway, the minimalist, would softly suggest that you *live with only what serves you.*

And your grandmother? She wouldn't use any of those words. She'd just say *make it home.*

Five people. Five different ways of saying the same thing: the daily, deeply personal work of surrounding yourself and your family with what you need to feel safe, comfortable, connected, and fully alive in the kind of home where you can kick off your shoes, breathe easy, and feel like you belong.

This chapter covers the full range of what access makes possible, and it's wider than most people expect. Furniture and appliances, yes. But also tires, technology, musical instruments and mobility devices. Even the storage building that gives your small business its first real home or the e-bike that gets you to work with the wind in your hair. If it's something a real family needs to live well, work steadily, or simply keep moving, there's a good chance access can get it through the door.

All of it. Accessed, not owned. Enjoyed, not anchored to.

That's what it really means to feather your nest in the fullest, most honest sense.

> Explore some real stories from the pages of this book: Robert's sofa meant more than comfort. It held a whole chapter of his life together. See Chapter 8. And for Cindy, a teal couch was the first thing that made her new home feel like hers. See Chapter 10.

The Toy Train in the Window

Do you remember the feeling?

Nose pressed against the cold glass, breath fogging the window, eyes locked on something that seemed — in that moment — like the most wonderful thing in the world. The toy train circling endlessly through the display. The bicycle with the chrome handlebars. The thing you were absolutely, completely, without-any-doubt certain would make your life better if only you could bring it home.

We never entirely outgrow that feeling. We just upgrade the window.

Now the display cases are everywhere. They're on your phone at midnight, in the store you ducked into for something else, in the neighbor's driveway, in the advertisement that followed you across three different websites. Today's shiny objects are more numerous, more sophisticated, and more persuasively marketed than anything a department store window could have ever managed. And that certainty we feel about them, that this one, this particular thing, will be the one that changes everything, is just as powerful at age forty-five as it was for that seven-year-old.

The treadmill you swore you'd use every morning. The stand mixer that was going to turn you into a baker. The massage chair that felt transformative in the showroom. The e-bike you pictured riding to work, scooting around traffic jams, saving money and getting fit. The big-screen television that seemed essential until you realized you watch everything on your laptop anyway.

We have all brought something home with complete conviction and discovered, three months later, that it had slowly become a very expensive coat rack.

Here is what nobody tells you at the point of purchase: ownership is a permanent answer to what might turn out to be a temporary question. The question is whether this thing, this particular object you're so certain about right now, will truly deliver the life improvement you're imagining. And more often than you'd like to admit, the honest answer is that it might — but you just don't know yet.

Rent-to-own changes that equation completely.

You don't have to guess. You don't have to commit. You don't have to lock-in years of payments for something you haven't tested yet. You bring it home. You live with it. You find out if you actually use that treadmill for all its benefits or if it just becomes a monument to good intentions. You find out whether the e-bike transforms your mornings or sits in the garage after the third rainy week. You find out whether the big screen truly changes your entertainment experience or whether you just comfortably revert back to watching everything on your familiar laptop as before.

And here is the part that makes this genuinely different from any other way of shopping: if the answer is no, if the thing doesn't deliver what you imagined, if the thrill fades, if your life is roughly the same with it as without it — you return it. Cleanly. Without guilt. Without a Facebook Marketplace listing you'll never get around to posting. Without absorbing the depreciation that is inevitable on something that didn't earn its place in your life.

Again, Seth Godin makes a powerful case in another of his books, *The Dip,* that the most successful plan is knowing when to quit. Instead of staying locked into something just because you've already invested in it, you release what no longer serves you to move toward what does. Lease-to-own embodies this wisdom: you're never trapped. You can return what no longer fits your life and step lightly into the next season.

But if the answer is yes. If you find yourself six weeks in and genuinely cannot picture your life without it, if it has delivered on your hopes and you could not bring yourself to return it, if it has earned its permanent place in your daily routine, then you keep making payments. And one day it's yours. Not because you were certain at the point of purchase.

Because you found out it was as great as you had imagined it would be.

That is not a compromise version of ownership. That is a smarter path to it.

The toy train in the window might be everything you imagined.

Rent-to-own is the smartest way to find out whether it belongs under your Christmas tree for good.

When the Fridge Gives Up the Ghost

Some things in life simply can't wait.

A functioning refrigerator isn't a luxury. It's the thing that keeps food chilled, medications safe, and your family's sense of normalcy intact. When you open the door to a strange odor, right before the kids need breakfast and you have to be at work early, it's not an inconvenience. It's an emergency.

The same goes for the furnace that quits in the middle of February or the air conditioner that gives out during a scorching July heat wave. These aren't minor household problems. They're moments when your home stops working for you, and suddenly you're scrambling.

Lease-to-own puts a quality brand-name appliance in your home today. Not next week, not after you've saved for months, not after a credit application that might get denied. You get it on terms that match your actual cash flow, with a clear path to own it later if you want.

That's not a lesser way to get a refrigerator. For millions of families, it's simply the way that keeps life moving when everything else has come to a sudden stop.

> Caroline experienced that feeling firsthand. One phone call changed everything for her family. *See Chapter 5.*

Safe Tires Are Not a Luxury

A tire isn't a comfort item. It is not a convenience. It's the crucial component that gets you where you need to be. Without safe and reliable transportation, you don't make it to your job and source of income on time. Your kids are not delivered to school or to a doctor's visit. You can't get your groceries onto your family table. It's also the single point of contact between a vehicle and the road, and when it fails, the consequences can be immediate, serious, and irreversible.

If you decide to take the chance and make it just a little longer on those worn tires, it's never because you don't care. It's because money is tight and replacing them just feels impossible.

RNR Tire Express, founded by Larry Sutton, built a national brand around one simple conviction: safe tires should be accessible to every driver, regardless of credit history or immediate cash on hand. Almost from the beginning, their guiding idea was "Serve, not service," and treating customers with genuine care and respect instead of just processing a transaction. With their "Everyone's Approved" approach, flexible weekly or monthly payments, and a Customer Care Package that often includes free installation, flat repairs, rotations, balance, lifetime alignment checks and sometimes even roadside assistance, RNR has turned tire replacement from a scary crisis into a manageable, dignified experience.

People shouldn't have to drive on unsafe tires simply because they can't afford the full replacement price today. Done right, lease-to-own makes sure they don't have to.

> Sheila experienced that philosophy first-hand when Kenny served her with respect, offering the dignity of a solution she could handle on her waitress pay. Calvin knew a delivery driver without dependable tires is a driver without an income. *See both stories in Chapter 8.*

Starting from Square One

There is a particular moment in American life that arrives for millions of young adults. The move into a first place. A lease signed. Keys in hand. And a completely empty space that somehow needs to become a functioning home before the first day of classes or the first morning of a new job.

The conventional options are familiar and mostly inadequate. Parents may contribute what they can spare. Secondhand furniture is hauled from wherever it can be found. Air mattresses substitute for beds. Milk crates become shelving. It is a rite of passage that most young adults accept as inevitable — and it is entirely unnecessary.

A graduate student or young adult with no credit history, limited savings, but does have a job, is precisely the consumer that rent-to-own was built to serve. It asks nothing of your credit file. It asks nothing of your savings beyond payments that fit a weekly or bi-weekly budget. This is exactly what would benefit a young person who might move again in twelve months.

The first home does not have to start from a blank space. It can start as furnished with the basics and livable from day one, and on terms that fit real life.

Kayla and Damon lived that exact moment — a new city, an empty living space, and two people who saw the solution differently until lease-to-own gave them both what they needed. *See Chapter 4.*

Heating and Cooling Your Home

The same logic extends to the home systems that most people never think about until the moment they fail. A furnace that stops in February or a central air conditioner that quits in the middle of a July heat advisory is not an inconvenience. It is a health emergency, particularly for the elderly, for young children, and for households in climates where temperature extremes are genuinely dangerous.

There are companies, Microf is one example, that have extended the lease-to-own model into HVAC systems. These companies coordinate through networks of licensed contractors to put a functioning heating or cooling system into a home on the same flexible, no-credit-needed terms that define the rest of the model. The product arrives installed and operational. The payment fits the household's actual cash flow. And the principle is identical to what applies to the refrigerator: no family should go without heat in winter or air conditioning in a dangerous summer simply because they cannot absorb the full replacement cost of a major home system today.

Self-Storage in Your Own Backyard

The access model has even reached backyards across America, which is one of the most overlooked categories.

Portable storage buildings and sheds, delivered directly to a customer's property and installed on-site, are available through lease-to-own programs from a multitude of local providers and hundreds of regional dealers organized through the National Shed Rental Association, many of whom are APRO members.

There are more than 50,000 self-storage facilities across the United States. This is more locations than all Subway, Dollar General, and CVS stores combined. Americans are paying to store their things at a rate that has made self-storage one of the most profitable industries in the country. The industry rakes $45–$48 billion every year and average folks are paying these billions month after month for space in structures they will never own, often miles from home. Could be that is what they want. But maybe, just maybe, they haven't thought there was an alternative.

A lease-to-own shed flips that script. The monthly payment is often comparable to what you were already spending on off-site storage. But now the building sits on your land, accessible anytime you need it. You can trade up to a larger size as your needs grow, pay off early with no penalty, or return it cleanly if your circumstances change. And if you keep making payments, one day it's yours, already installed on your property.

That's access applied to the very problem that endless ownership tends to create.

> Marcus found out what having his own space meant for building something from the ground up. *See Chapter 6.*

Getting a Jump on Obsolescence

Technology moves so fast that outright purchase often feels like buying yesterday's news. The television you buy today will be surpassed by a better, cheaper model within eighteen months. The laptop you invest in will feel slow within three years. The gaming console or home audio system that represents the current state of the art today will be two generations behind before the financing is even paid off.

The day you buy electronics, you also buy the inevitable obsolescence. It comes with the receipt.

Lease-to-own offers something traditional retail cannot. The ability to access current technology without absorbing the full depreciation curve of a rapidly evolving product. You use it. You enjoy it. When something meaningfully better appears on the horizon, your agreement gives you a path to that improved version. Before, your perfectly good, yet inferior, item would have gone into the back of your closet or you might have sold it for a fraction of what you paid. With LTO, you can stay cutting edge. You never own the obsolescence.

For a generation that has grown up treating technology as a service rather than an asset, streaming instead of buying, subscribing instead of owning, this feels completely natural. The television on the wall, the laptop on the desk, the tablet in the kitchen: accessed, enjoyed, and upgraded when life moves on.

> Jasmine spent an entire Saturday in the August heat hauling her friend's stuff down four flights of stairs and made a decision that changed how she thought about owning things forever. *See Chapter 16.*

RTO Longevity — Musical Instruments

Long before the subscription economy had a name. Long before Netflix and Spotify rewired consumer expectations. Long before anyone had written a business school case study about access versus ownership. Millions of American families were already living the principle consistently, naturally and without a second thought.

Every September, a letter made its way home, often tucked in a school backpack or delivered by the postman, and landed on kitchen tables across the country. It announced the start of band or orchestra season. And tucked inside, almost always, was a flyer from the local music shop explaining their rental program. Month to month. No long-term commitment. Apply your payments toward a acquiring ownership if you decide to keep it.

That was rent-to-own. It always has been. And nobody questioned it, because nobody needed to.

Personal Mobility — Gen-Z to Golden Age

If musical instruments are the most established expression of the lease-to-own mindset, the rapidly expanding world of personal mobility zips into its newest and most cutting edge spot. One that spans an extraordinary range of needs, abilities, and life circumstances.

At one end of that spectrum sits the e-bike. For urban Millennials and Gen Z, it is the physical embodiment of the access mindset applied to personal transportation, lightweight, nimble, sustainable, and liberating. Lease-to-own programs from providers under many brand names have made the e-bike accessible on exactly the flexible terms that this generation expects from every other product category in their lives.

For Baby Boomers, the e-bike tells a different but equally compelling story. The step-through frame designs now standard on many models were engineered with the older rider in mind. The pedal-assist technology means that the ride is as strenuous or as gentle as the rider chooses. This can be therapeutic for older adults managing the physical realities of aging without surrendering to them.

At the other end are powered mobility devices that many people only think about when they or someone they care for has that need arise. Lease-to-own options keep people independent, active, and engaged at the stages of life when independence matters most. And when a physician prescribes a device as medically necessary, Medicare can often help cover a significant portion while lease-to-own bridges any gaps.

Access Where Life Happens

Step back and look at everything this chapter has covered: home furnishings, appliances, electronics, tires, storage buildings, musical instruments, e-bikes, and the full spectrum of personal mobility devices. You see that a pattern emerges that is both simple and profound.

In every category, lease-to-own does the same essential thing: It takes something people genuinely need, whether for safety, comfort, dignity, independence, their children's education, or simple quality of life, and makes it available right now to people who need it today but can't acquire it outright.

That's more than a transaction. It touches something deeply human.

And the people who use it, the family whose refrigerator died on a weeknight, the parent renting a clarinet for a ten-year-old who might become a musician, the young professional choosing an e-bike instead of a second car, the retired teacher leasing a mobility scooter because she refuses to let age slow her down, are all living some version of the same silent truth.

> And sometimes, lease-to-own does something even more profound than solve a

> practical problem. For Pam and George, the first "*yes*" after months of "*no*" gave them back something they thought they had lost. *See Chap. 7.*

It was never about holding a cash receipt. It was always about a home that worked, a life that fit, and the freedom to change course whenever life presented the option.

* * *

Chapter 4

Two People — One Smart Decision

Moving in together is not only a big step, but more often than not, a chance to discover new things about each other.

Not the lease signing, though that is no small thing. Not the address change or the shared mailbox or figuring out whose name goes first on the utilities. The real step is this: two people who have been living their own separate lives, making their own separate decisions, suddenly have to make most every decision considering another's wishes. Including the ones about money.

Kayla and Damon found out standing in empty rooms in a city where neither of them knew a single person.

Kayla and Damon

They had been couple for two years before they decided to make the move. Both mid-twenties. Both with real jobs and real paychecks. Both ready, or at least they thought they were ready, for the next chapter.

Getting there had not been a perfectly straight line for Damon. Like a lot of college students, he had been flooded with credit card offers the moment he set foot on campus. It felt like free money at the time. Pizza. Concert tickets. A spring break he probably didn't need. By the time he graduated he was carrying more debt than his first salary could comfortably handle, and the credit score that followed him out the door reflected every one of those decisions. He had spent three years digging out. The hole was almost filled in, but almost wasn't the same as done.

Damon had gotten a job as a trucking dispatcher in a town about two hours away from where they had both been living. He felt like it was a good opportunity. A place he could grow. The kind of offer you say yes to even when it means uprooting everything. Kayla worked remote for her company, so there was nothing to keep her from moving to where he needed to be. They signed a lease on a Saturday, drove up the next day, and had carted everything they owned between them inside their new place by three in the afternoon.

Beyond their few pieces of furniture, they were surrounded by just boxes, bare floors, and that funny echo of a space that has not become a home yet.

Kayla looked around the living room and felt the pull immediately. She knew exactly what this space could be. She had been thinking about it on the drive. Their couch could go against that wall, but they needed a rug to warm up the floors. Some curtains. Some kind of lighting that didn't come from a single bare bulb in the ceiling. Her challenge was to make it feel like their place in this city where she didn't know a single street or a single face. This task was the one thing she knew she could tackle. Yes, she could handle this.

Damon looked around the same room and felt something different. Caution, maybe? Hesitancy, for sure.

The job was good, but it was new. The city was unfamiliar. The lease was twelve months, which felt manageable, but in that short time there would be decisions about what was to come next, and he didn't know what came next. He had watched friends load moving trucks twice in three years, hauling furniture purchased for one life that didn't quite fit it in the next one. He didn't want that. He wasn't wanting to be difficult. He was trying to be smart.

So when Kayla said she wanted to go look at room accessories that afternoon, Damon said, “Let’s wait.”

Kayla twisted her mouth to the side and replied, “You really wanna eat dinner perched on the sofa?”

“It’s only temporary.” He said with a grin.

Kayla sighed, “But I don’t want home to feel temporary.”

That conversation went on for a while. Neither of them was wrong. They were just standing in the same nearly empty room and seeing two completely different things.

The Third Option

They almost went to bed that night without resolving anything. Boxes still unpacked, takeout containers on the kitchen counter, the echo still in the walls.

But Kayla had been reading about lease-to-own and mentioned it the way you mention something you are not quite sure will land.

Sitting cross-legged on the sofa, Kayla turned to face him.

"You remember my friend, Jordan? The one who showed up to my cousin's wedding in those ridiculous plaid pants?" She didn’t wait for an answer. “Anyway, he got a full scholarship to State.

Giant campus, twelve hundred acres, and he was spending thirty minutes walking to his next class rather than admit he was losing valuable time. Too proud for the bus. Too broke for a car."

Damon smiled a little, remembering the plaid pants.

"So he walks into a lease-to-own store near campus one day, completely on a whim, and walks out with an e-bike. Leased it. Weekly payments that fit his teaching assistant budget. He rode that thing everywhere for two years. I mean everywhere. Showed up to things with helmet hair and didn't care at all." She laughed at the memory. "Then he gets this incredible fellowship across the country and you know what he did? Rode the bike back to the store. Handed it over. That was it. Paid for the time he used it and nothing else. No storage unit. No selling it to some stranger on Facebook. Clean."

She looked at Damon.

"That always stayed with me. The way it just ended when he was done with it."

Damon had questions. Reasonable ones. How do the payments work. What happens if they move. What happens if something breaks.

The answers turned out to be simpler than he expected.

With lease-to-own, they could get real furnishings, like rugs, lamps, end tables, coffee table and pictures for the walls. Maybe a chair to sit across from their sofa. Weekly or monthly payments that fit their actual budget. And if the city didn't work out, if the job changed, if life went somewhere neither of them had planned for, they could return the items and walk away from the lease account cleanly. No debt chasing them. No trailer full of things that no longer fit their life.

Damon went silent for a moment. Kayla knew what that meant. The quiet contemplative Damon was emerging. That Damon always crept up when something was making sense to him.

Kayla waited.

He said: so we get the place the way you want it, and if we need to move on, we are not stuck with any of it.

She said: that is exactly right.

He thought about it a little longer. Then he said with a sheepish grin, "I can't believe I'm saying this, but it makes perfect sense. I'm in."

That was a Sunday night. By Tuesday evening there was a rug on those floors, a new occasional chair, canvas prints on the wall, and a lamp in the corner that made the whole room feel warm. Kayla walked in from the kitchen with two cups of coffee and handed one to Damon. They sat in their new surrounds in the calm of their new town and their home didn't echo anymore.

It felt like theirs.

What Kayla and Damon Got Right

They didn't just furnish rooms. They found a way to honor both of their instincts at the same time.

Kayla's instinct was right. A home that feels like home changes how you feel about everything around it. When you walk into a space at the end of a long day in an unfamiliar city and the space feels warm and real and yours, that matters. Comfort is not a luxury. Belonging is not a luxury. Kayla knew that, and she was right to know it.

Damon's instinct was right too. Overcommitting to things in a situation that is still finding its shape is how people end up stuck. Buying furnishings on credit in a city you have never lived in before, for a job you have only had for a few weeks, is a reasonable thing to be cautious about. His hesitation wasn't stubbornness. It was good judgment.

Lease-to-own didn't ask either of them to give up their instinct. It just gave both instincts a place to stand at the same time.

That outcome isn't always easy to find. In most financial decisions, one person has to win the argument and one person has to let something go. Kayla and Damon found a way where neither of them had to lose.

Eighteen months later, Damon is still at the same firm. The city has become familiar in the way cities do when you stop being a visitor and start being a resident. They know their coffee shop and their dry cleaner and the shortcut that saves seven minutes on the way home.

And the furnishings and accessories? About six months in, when the job felt solid and the city felt like home, they chose the option in their rental-purchase agreement to acquire ownership. That is something worth understanding about how most people use lease-to-own in their lives. Most folks don't ride the agreement to the end of the full term. When their cash flow allows, they choose to acquire ownership early, often at a meaningful savings off the total cost. The items become theirs on their timeline, not a fixed schedule somebody else set. Kayla and Damon did exactly that. The chair is theirs. The rug is theirs. The lamp in the corner that made the room feel warm on a Tuesday night in a town where they didn't know anyone is still in that same corner.

But if the story had gone differently, if the job had not worked out or the city had not fit, they would have made a phone call and two guys would have come and carried the items out the same way they carried them in.

No moving truck. No debt. No argument about whose fault it was.

Just two people, ready for whatever is on the horizon.

* * *

Chapter 5

Meeting Folks Where They Live

The rent-to-own store on the main street of small-town America rarely gets the credit it deserves.

It doesn't look flashy. It doesn't run national ad campaigns with celebrities. But for decades it has constantly done something most big retailers won't: it says "yes" when almost everyone else has said "no."

This chapter isn't about perfect financial theory. It's about real people walking through real doors on real days when life got heavy, and finding a way forward anyway.

It's Cold Milk — Not the Fridge

Caroline stood at the sink that warm Indiana evening, the dishwater long gone cold, her feet throbbing after another double shift. She pulled open the refrigerator door and wrinkled her nose at the sour smell of spoiled milk. The kids would need breakfast in the morning, but the carton sat there like a small betrayal.

She had two little ones who needed breakfast before school, a job that started early, and a paycheck that barely stretched to the end of the month. There was certainly no cash for a new refrigerator, and her credit score had taken a hit during a rough divorce two years earlier.

Before she finally crawled into bed that night, she carried all those pricey groceries out to the trash can. The next morning, she guiltily handed each of the kids a Pop Tart, dropped them at school, called her boss to request the morning off, and drove to the big-box store, hoping for a miracle. The salesman ran her credit and shook his head. "Sorry, not approved today." She tried another store. Same story.

By 11:15 a.m. her awful morning took an unexpected turn. She walked into the last stop on her list — the little rent-to-own store she had never visited before. They didn't ask to run her credit. They only wanted to know what she was shopping for and whether she had a steady job.

Twenty minutes later, Caroline was giving them her address for same-day delivery. She stood there speechless. In addition to the giant knot unraveling in her stomach, she felt a wave of relief, amazement, gratitude, and a fleeting worry that she might still be dreaming.

When her head finally hit the pillow that night, she dropped right off to sleep. Her kids would wake up to safe, cold milk in the morning.

That wasn't a luxury story. That was a dignity story.

The rent-to-own model didn't solve every problem in her life. But it solved the immediate one without ever making her feel small in the process.

> "*People don't want what you make. They want what it will do for them. They want the way it will make them feel.*" - Seth Godin, author and veteran podcaster

Caroline didn't want a refrigerator. It was the cold milk she really wanted, along with the relief it brought her.

Where Standard Retail Often Fails

Walk into most big retailers and the process is familiar: pick the item, apply for financing, wait for approval. If your credit is thin, damaged, or simply nonexistent, the conversation ends quickly. "Sorry, we can't help you today."

For millions of responsible, working Americans, especially in rural areas or after a job loss, medical bill, or divorce, that door stays closed.

Rent-to-own stores operate differently. They don't check credit the same way. They focus on whether you have steady income and can make the next payment. They understand that life is messy and circumstances change. Most importantly, they're set up to deliver the product today, install it if needed, and include service and maintenance as part of the standard agreement.

They meet people where they actually live, not where the perfect financial spreadsheet says they should be.

The Communities the Map Forgot

There's a side of America that many people never see on a regular map. Places where the nearest bank branch is more than ten miles away. These are called banking deserts, and there are thousands of them across the country, mostly in rural areas in the South, Appalachia, the Great Plains, and the rural Southwest.

For families living there, the lack of a nearby bank isn't just annoying. It creates real barriers. Without easy access to a bank, it's much harder to build a credit history or score. And without those, the usual financing options that many other Americans rely on for appliances, furniture, or safe vehicles simply aren't available.

It's getting tougher. Since 2009, the U.S. has lost thousands of bank branches, with the losses hitting rural and lower-income areas especially hard. Imagine waking up to find the bank on Main Street has closed its doors. The place where you cashed your paycheck and talked to someone who knew your name and recognized your face. No warning, no nearby replacement, just a notice on the window pointing to a distant call center. For a family in a small town, that closure means longer drives, no easy place to handle daily or weekly banking, and one more connection to the wider financial world just slipping away.

Rural communities are far more likely to face this situation than cities or suburbs. The well-known study, mentioned in Chapter 2, of nearly 3,000 rent-to-own customers showed that 68 percent lived in rural areas or small towns, not in big cities with stores on every corner. These are the places where the usual financial map has left gaps.

In small towns across rural Missouri, the hills of Appalachia, or the brush country of South Texas, local RTO stores often serve as steady anchors on Main Street. Many are independent operators who've been there for years. Others belong to nationwide companies that still value personal service, with folks who greet you by name, understand the rhythms of the community, and show up consistently. Names you might recognize include Aaron's, Rent-A-Center, RNR Tire Express, and thousands of hometown stores that never stopped serving the neighborhoods the bigger financial world walked away from.

When something breaks in these communities, like a refrigerator on a Sunday night, a washing machine before school starts, or tires that are barely even safe for the road, the nearest big-box store can be forty miles and hours away. That distance isn't just a number. It's a real hardship. This is why the promise of "take it home today," "delivered when you need it," and "installed before we leave" means so much. In these towns, those aren't just nice words. They're often a true lifeline that local rent-to-own stores have dependably kept for decades.

Shop Local: RTO in Your Neighborhood

There's something special about the rent-to-own stores that stayed open even during the tough times like the 2008 crash. The ones where the owner knows your name, remembers your paycheck schedule, and genuinely asks how your kids are doing.

Most of these stores aren't run by some big corporation from far away. They're small, local family businesses, often passed down through generations. They were started by folks who took a big chance on one storefront in one neighborhood and have been consistently showing up for their community ever since. They hire local people, buy from American suppliers, and when you make a payment there, a good chunk of that money stays right in your town paying wages, covering taxes, and helping other nearby businesses stay open.

This fits perfectly with the "shop local" spirit so many of us believe in. Think about the local hardware store, the corner diner, or the independent pharmacy. They don't just sell stuff. They sponsor the kids' sports teams, give a first job to the teenager down the street, and stick around through good times and bad. The independent rent-to-own stores belong in that same group. These aren't shady operators. They're productive American small business owners who saw a real need in their community and stepped up to fill it. They follow the rules, belong to professional groups that keep standards high, and earn customer loyalty the old-fashioned way: by being there year after year.

And there's something you just can't get from a big chain or an app. When the owner knows your name, knows when payday is, and checks in after dropping off your new refrigerator or washer, that's not just good service. That's what happens when a business is run by real people who know and care about their neighbors. The trust feels different because it's built face-to-face, over time, in your own community. That's something worth supporting, not just because it helps you, but because it helps everyone around you too.

When Everything You Own Is Swept Away

There is a category of human experience that no financial system was designed to address. The moment when a family loses not just one essential item, but everything. A house fire. A flood. A tornado that takes the roof and everything beneath it. A hurricane that erases an entire neighborhood overnight.

In those moments, FEMA assistance is measured in weeks. Insurance claims are measured in months. And a family that is displaced, traumatized, and starting from zero needs a functioning household today. Not when the paperwork clears. Not when the adjuster files the report. Today.

The rent-to-own model is one of the very few consumer arrangements built to meet that need at that speed. Same-day delivery. No credit needed. A refrigerator that chills, a bed that provides rest for the weary, a washer for the clothes donated by neighbors, all of it accessible within hours of walking through the door, on payment terms that fit whatever the family can manage in that moment.

Across the Gulf Coast, through Tornado Alley, in the flood plains of the Midwest and the fire corridors of the West, RTO stores have dependably served as first responders of a particular kind — not with emergency services, but with the dignity of a functioning home. It is not a role the industry promotes loudly. But it is a role it has filled, steadily and without fanfare, every time a community has needed it.

Welcomed, Approved, and Included

There is something that Dr. Smitherman captures in his book that no purely financial argument about the lease-to-own model has ever quite managed to convey, and it deserves to be said plainly here, in the chapter most concerned with the people it serves most deeply.

For families that have spent years navigating a financial system designed to exclude them, those turned away by banks, rejected by credit applications, treated as risks rather than customers, the experience of walking into an RTO store is not simply a business exchange. It is something more personal and more significant than that. It is the experience of being welcomed.

Dr. Smitherman writes that for families excluded from credit, the ability to walk into an RTO store means entering "a space where they are welcomed, approved, and included," without the fear of rejection that conventional retail and traditional lending have made a routine indignity of their financial lives.

Think about what that means in human terms. Every "no" from the bank, the credit card company, the appliance store's financing desk, adds a little more weight on their shoulders, until it compounds into something heavier than any single rejection should carry. After enough credit checks and polite refusals that seem to overlook who they really are and how responsibly they live, it's easy to feel discouraged, even to wonder if the system sees them as somehow "less."

Then they walk into a modern rent-to-own store and are told something refreshingly positive. No credit needed. No score that fails to capture their real life or their responsible habits. Just a clear, respectful path forward with the freedom to bring home what they need today.

That yes is not a marketing strategy. It is the fundamental operating principle of a model that was built, from its origins in the 1960s, around the conviction that every family deserves access to the essentials of a decent life, regardless of what a credit algorithm says about them. For many, it was the first time they felt truly respected and valued. The first time the folks at a store felt genuinely glad to see them. And for the families who had heard nothing but no for years, that yes was everything.

If you have read anything negative about rent-to-own online and found yourself wondering, we address those questions honestly and directly in the back of this book, in a section titled "How Skeptics Forged a Superior RTO." It is there for the reader who wants the full picture, including where the industry has genuinely improved and where the criticism was fair. The story is more nuanced, yet more encouraging, than most headlines suggest.

If You Could Step Back in Time

Imagine jumping into Marty McFly's DeLorean, punching in 1985, and walking into a rent-to-own store from that era. Then imagine stepping back into today. The difference would take your breath away.

Back then, information was scarce, terms were often unclear, and the whole process could feel uncertain. Today, most providers offer clean, easy-to-read agreements that explain costs and rights in plain English. You can review everything before ever signing a thing. The entire experience has shifted, gently but unmistakably, in the customer's favor.

Some companies have gone even further. RNR Tire Express built its own paperless system from the ground up, designed specifically around the way real families live and make decisions. Most stores allow you to align your payment date with your actual paycheck. A small adjustment that costs the company nothing but gives you one less thing to worry about. When something breaks, help is usually just a phone call away, with no extra charge and no long wait.

The promise of "no worries" isn't just a marketing phrase. For many families, it's a promise that's actually kept.

What to Watch For

Not every rent-to-own store operates the way the best ones do. This book would not be honest if it pretended otherwise.

Teresa found this out the hard way. A single mother in a mid-sized Southern city, she walked into an RTO store she'd seen advertised on a bus shelter and left with a laptop for her daughter's first year of high school. The payments seemed manageable. But the paperwork she signed was dense with language she didn't fully understand, and when she asked questions, the associate moved quickly past them.

Two months in, she missed a payment during a particularly tight week and the phone calls started the next day. Not one call. Several. When she returned the laptop voluntarily, she was told her payments were simply lost. No reinstatement explained, no path back offered. She felt ashamed and confused, certain she had done something wrong.

She hadn't. The store had not been affiliated with APRO, had no reinstatement policy on record, and had made no effort to explain her rights. What Teresa experienced wasn't rent-to-own as this book describes it. It was a version of it. One operating at the edges of the model, without the standards or accountability that reputable operators maintain.

Her story is the reason this book exists alongside the *Four Core Truths*. A good operator welcomes your questions before you sign. A good operator explains reinstatement before you need it. A good operator will never make you feel that a missed payment is a moral failure. If the store you are considering can't clearly answer the questions in Chapter 9, walk out the door and find one that can. They exist. And they have been dependably earning the trust of families like Teresa's for decades.

* * *

Chapter 6

Walking it Back

When Marcus launched his business, he was living in a small mobile home outside town on a few acres his uncle helped him find years earlier. It wasn't fancy, but it was his. Gravel driveway. Chain-link fence. Enough room to park equipment without neighbors complaining.

The first thing he added was a portable storage building behind the house.

At first it held a mower, trimmers, fuel cans, and hand tools. Then came shelving systems because landscaping businesses collect things quickly. Irrigation parts. Spare blades. Boxes of fittings. Equipment manuals. Eventually he added a small office setup too. Computer. Printer. Whiteboard calendar. Filing cabinet. The little systems that transform side work into a real company.

The portable building, shelving systems, and office equipment all came through lease-to-own arrangements.

At the time, that decision barely registered as important.

He needed infrastructure before he needed ownership.

On summer evenings, Marcus sometimes stood outside after unloading equipment and looked at the storage building with its floodlight glowing above the door.

It looked like progress.

When the business closed, unwinding everything hurt almost as much as building it had felt good.

The stand-on mower sold to a friend in the business.

The aerator sold on Facebook.

The enclosed trailer with his company logo on both sides even sold.

Customers stopped calling.

The yard slowly looked bigger.

The portable building emptied slowly.

Marcus stood inside one evening surrounded by empty shelves and dusty floor outlines where equipment had been sitting. His footsteps echoed now. That surprised him. He had spent so many evenings in that building organizing jobs for the next morning that silence felt wrong.

What surprised him more was how simple the next part became.

The shelving returned.

The office equipment returned.

The portable storage building was picked up.

No classified ads. No strangers showing up late. No trying to recover pennies on the dollar from infrastructure purchased for a version of life that no longer existed.

Within a few weeks, the space behind the house was empty again except for gravel, tire tracks, and a patch of grass that had never seen sunlight.

Marcus hated that.

He also needed it.

Marcus found work again faster than expected. Within three months, a regional landscaping company hired him as an operations manager. The paycheck returned. Benefits returned. Every Friday, direct deposit landed in his account again.

That steady paycheck brought relief.

More importantly, it brought breathing room.

For almost two years, Marcus had measured time by invoices, weather forecasts, fuel prices, and whether enough customers had paid on schedule. Now somebody else worried about payroll and insurance renewals and whether rain delays would wreck the month.

He had forgotten what that felt like.

The first Saturday after taking the new job, Marcus woke up at six out of habit, pulled on work boots, stepped outside with coffee, and looked toward the empty space behind his mobile home where the storage building used to sit.

For a moment, the emptiness bothered him. Then he realized something. Empty space can be loss, but it can also be open room.

Months later, Marcus started approaching purchases differently. Not fearfully. Just differently. Now he wanted flexibility. He wanted options. He wanted fewer decisions that assumed life would cooperate forever.

Lease-to-own finally made sense to him then. Not because things were going badly anymore, but because he finally understood how quickly good plans can change. The portable building had helped him grow when growth mattered. Returning it had helped him shrink when shrinking mattered.

That flexibility brought relief. Almost a calm. Because trying again someday suddenly felt possible.

What Marcus Learned

Marcus will tell you he would still take the chance. Maybe not every decision exactly the same way. Maybe with more cushion. Maybe with fewer assumptions about weather patterns and commercial contracts. But he would still try.

Because being wrong about how something turns out is not the same thing as making the wrong decision.

His footing came back. His confidence came back. His willingness to build something again came back too.

Slower this time. Steadier.

These days, if you drive past his place outside town, you will still see trailers parked in the driveway sometimes. You will still see stacks of pavers near the fence and muddy boots by the back steps.

The empty space behind the house eventually stopped looking like failure. It started looking like extra room. Room for whatever came next.

And for the first time in a long while, Marcus had

started looking at that empty space the same way landscapers look at bare ground.

Not for what was missing.

For what could grow there next.

* * *

Chapter 7

Starting Over From Nothing

Some people lose their financial footing because they made bad decisions.

That is not Pam and George's story.

Pam and George lost their financial footing because their daughter became terribly ill. And when your child is sick, you don't sit down and run spreadsheets. You do what parents do. You show up. You fight. You sign whatever needs to be signed and figure out the rest later.

The rest came later. And it was hard.

But this chapter is not really about how the grounded life they had built just crumbled away. It is about how they got it back. And about the reliable and practical tool that helped them do it with their heads held high.

Pam and George

They had been married seventeen years when their daughter Lily was diagnosed.

Lily was eleven—still young enough to leave wet towels on the bathroom floor and old enough to roll her eyes when Pam kissed the top of her head in front of friends. The diagnosis came on a Tuesday afternoon beneath fluorescent lights that buzzed softly overhead. There were four doctors, a social worker, a stack of forms thick enough to feel important, and a small conference room that smelled faintly of disinfectant, burnt coffee, and the kind of clean air hospitals seemed to manufacture to hide the fear.

Pam couldn't remember much of what was said after the first few sentences.

Serious. Aggressive. Treatment plan.

George reached across the table and took her hand. She noticed then how cold his fingers were.

Later, neither of them could remember leaving the room.

What followed wasn't one tough season but hundreds of tough days strung together so tightly they eventually stopped trying to separate them. Two years of hospital rooms where mornings and evenings looked the same. Two years of specialist visits, medication schedules taped to refrigerators, insurance approvals that arrived too late, and bills that arrived right on time.

Pam took leave from work because there were weeks when Lily needed her every minute. George picked up extra shifts because somebody had to pay for the parts insurance didn't touch—the hotel rooms near specialists, the prescriptions that somehow weren't covered, the meals from vending machines eaten at midnight.

Exhaustion became so ordinary they stopped mentioning it.

And grief, real grief, did strange things to memory.

Sitting beside Lily during long treatments, Pam would suddenly think of her mother in those final months years earlier: the slow shrinking of a woman who had once seemed permanent, the way illness silently stole pieces before it took the whole person. She had spent years learning not to think about those memories. Now they arrived uninvited.

George had his own ghosts.

Driving home after twelve-hour shifts, he sometimes found himself thinking about his friend Mark, who had spent three years losing a battle with his lungs one breath at a time. He remembered hospital parking lots. The smell of antiseptic. The helpless anger of watching someone you love become smaller inside their own body.

But there were other thoughts too—the ones he tried hardest to push away.

Long before Lily was born, before the mortgage and school pickups and dance recitals, George had carried around a hopeful picture of the future the way most fathers do without realizing it. He had imagined standing at the back of a church one day watching his daughter turn the corner in a white dress. He had imagined pretending not to cry and failing at it anyway.

Sometimes, late at night driving home, he would grip the steering wheel and catch himself calculating years.

Eleven.

Twelve.

Thirteen.

Would there be sixteen? Would there be prom pictures taped to the refrigerator? Would there be the awkward moment when some nervous boy knocked on the front door?

And the thought he could never quite outrun: the father-daughter dance. He could see it so clearly it almost hurt—the music he didn't know yet, Lily laughing because he had no rhythm, her head resting against his shoulder for what would probably be the last time she would ever seem small.

The life George imagined for Lily had taken shape slowly over the years—so slowly he had forgotten those moments existed only in his heart.

The Cost After

Still, every morning they got up and did it again because parents learn quickly that fear becomes a luxury when your child still needs breakfast, medication, clean clothes, and someone willing to look them in the eyes and say, *You're going to be okay,* even on the days you are not sure you believe it yourself.

They had savings when all of this started. Not wealth. Just the kind of savings people build slowly over time through skipped vacations, automatic transfers every payday, and small sacrifices repeated often enough to become habits. They had an emergency fund. A little set aside for the future. Enough to make them feel responsible.

By the time Lily finished treatment and received her clean bill of health, it was gone.

Not wasted. Not spent recklessly. Gone. The way money disappears when your child needs another medication, another hotel room near a specialist, another unpaid week away from work, another thing insurance decides is not covered after all.

Lily was healthy. That remained the thing that mattered most. George would tell you that immediately and mean every word. But he would also tell you something else: surviving the crisis and surviving what comes afterward are not always the same thing.

When the appointments finally slowed down and life stopped revolving around treatment schedules, Pam and George opened accounts they had avoided looking at for months. The savings account showed numbers they barely recognized. Credit cards they had used to bridge impossible stretches now carried balances that felt permanent. During the most difficult months, accounts slipped behind because there simply wasn't enough money for everything. Responsible choices stopped meaning good choices and started meaning deciding which problem could wait until next month.

They had done everything parents are supposed to do. Life had simply cost more than they had.

The Nos

Lily came home healthy in the spring. By summer,

Pam and George were trying to remember what ordinary families did.

The house around them carried evidence of the last two years. The kitchen table had by necessity become command central—homework station, medication station, bill-paying station, late-night crying station. One leg wobbled enough that George automatically steadied it every time he sat down.

None of these things seemed important when compared to what they had survived. But homes absorb hardship. Eventually the worn places start reminding you of it.

Pam wanted to replace it. Nothing extravagant. Just a new table and chairs so they could stop looking at their kitchen table as a reminder of that soul-wrenching season of their lives.

George went to a furniture store after work one Tuesday. The credit application took four minutes. The answer took less than one.

He tried somewhere else the next day.

Same answer.

Driving home, he realized he had started dreading sales counters and automatic doors—the unavoidable humiliation of hoping before someone typed numbers into a screen.

That evening he sat at that old kitchen table and pressed his palm flat against the wobbling edge while Pam finished dishes nearby. She never asked how it went because she already knew.

After enough no's, something shifts. The first rejection stings. The second embarrasses. By the time you've lost count, it starts feeling personal — as if numbers on a screen have decided something about who you are. They haven't. But exhaustion has a way of making that fiction in your head feel true.

The Yes

After Church the next Sunday, while balancing a styrofoam coffee cup and making small talk in the fellowship hall, a long-time friend mentioned the lease-to-own store in town.

“Why don’t you check them out?” she said casually.

George nodded politely, changed the subject, and spent the next week thinking about it.

The following Saturday, they followed that friend’s tip and went together to the store.

Nobody asked them to explain their hardship. Nobody made faces at numbers. Nobody disappeared into an office leaving them standing in silence. The person behind the counter simply asked what they needed.

Needed.

Not what they qualified for.

What they needed.

Pam found a kitchen table with four chairs and legs that sat firmly on the floor without shifting. A table top that wasn't worn away or scratched up from those moments of frustration they had endured.

The payments fit their budget. The paperwork made sense. If something were to start wobbling, they would help. If life changed again—and both of them now understood how quickly life could change—they had options.

The table and chairs arrived right as scheduled and that evening looked ordinary in the way extraordinary things sometimes do. Lily spread homework across the new tabletop while Pam made spaghetti sauce in the kitchen and George sat on the couch pretending to read a book, but mostly just watching his family.

Nothing remarkable happened.

Which made it remarkable.

Because for the first time in years, the house felt like a place where normal Tuesdays could happen again.

Pam stood over the stove a little longer than necessary because tears kept appearing without permission. Not sadness. Relief. The strange, disorienting feeling of discovering there really can be a light at the end of the tunnel, after all.

What This Is Really About

Lease-to-own did not erase balances or magically refill savings accounts. It did not undo hospital rooms, fear, or two years spent wondering what tomorrow would bring.

What it did was smaller than that and somehow bigger too.

It gave them a yes at a moment when life had trained them to expect another no. It gave them a home that stopped looking like survival and started looking like living again.

About six months later, after overtime shifts, careful budgeting, and enough breathing room to think about the future again, Pam and George chose to acquire ownership. The table became theirs.

Lily still does homework there.

She is fourteen now and healthy. She has no idea what that table cost her parents—not the buyout amount, but the other cost. The one measured in hospital parking lots, emptied savings accounts, and nights spent doing math that never quite worked.

George would go through every day of it again without hesitation.

But he is glad the table is just the right size for homework and a family meal.

And he is glad somebody finally told them *yes*.

* * *

Chapter 8

Where the Yes Lives

Maria : Three Generations

Maria still remembers the exact day of 2003 when she pushed open the door of the little rent-to-own store in her Indiana town. Her young son clung to her legs while the winter wind bit at their backs. Money had always been tight, but that month it felt impossible. And now her stove had stopped heating weeks ago.

The store manager didn't treat her like a risk. He listened considerately, then walked her through the options with genuine kindness. No long forms, no credit judgment. Just a weekly payment she could manage from her paycheck and the promise that the new stove would arrive the next afternoon. When she saw the red glow of the burner element, Maria almost shouted out. A warm meal the first time in months, she could breathe again.

That single "yes" became the beginning of something much larger. Over the next twenty years, Maria turned to the same flexible model every time life shifted. She furnished three different homes as her family grew and moved. She replaced appliances when they wore out. Not with panic, but with calm planning. When her daughter left for her first place on her own, Maria walked beside her into the store and helped her pick out the basics: a sturdy couch, a microwave, a bed that would offer her a good night's sleep.

"It let me provide for my kids without the stress of big debt hanging over us," Maria says now, her voice warm with remembered relief. "It gave me dignity when I needed it most."

Today, Maria's granddaughter is doing the same thing. Stepping into her very first place as an adult with the same practical confidence her grandmother once carried. Three generations. One trusted tool. What started as a stove has become a sturdy thread of stability woven through their family's story. Maria doesn't see it as charity or a last resort. She sees it as proof that a working mother's love, paired with a fair and flexible option, can build something lasting. She is the hero of her own life, steady, resourceful, and fiercely protective of the people she loves.

Calvin's : Week by Week, Mile by Mile

Calvin drives a delivery route across Georgia six days a week. His truck is his livelihood. When two of his tires needed replacing, he knew he couldn't wait weeks to save up or risk another credit denial.

He stopped at an RNR Tire Express location. In almost no time, he was back on the road with safe, reliable tires and a payment plan that fit his weekly route paycheck. The service package he selected with the tires even included free rotations and flat repairs going forward.

Calvin later said, "A delivery driver without dependable tires is a man without income. They didn't treat me like a risk. They treated me like a guy trying to keep food on the table. That mattered more than the tires themselves."

Pratt Family : Generational Safety Net

In a small Oklahoma town, the three Pratt grandchildren were excited about moving into their first home on their own. One attending community college. The other two starting new jobs in construction. Their grandparents wanted to help them furnish their new place so they could focus on work and studies. They knew the importance of sleeping on a real bed instead of on bare floors.

The local rent-to-own store worked out a flexible plan the grandparents could manage alongside their fixed income. Beds, a small table, and a basic living room set arrived the week before classes started.

One of the three later sent the store a photo of them enjoying a meal at their new kitchen table. The note attached simply read: “Thank you for helping us start strong.”

A Built-In Peace of Mind Champion

When you enter into lease-to-own, you are not simply acquiring a product.

You are acquiring a champion.

That word champion is carefully and deliberately chosen. Not a vendor. Not a service provider. Not a company with whom you have done business. A champion. Someone who is actively on your side, who has a stake in your success, and who will show up when things go wrong rather than leaving you to figure it out alone.

This is what much of the industry calls the Customer Care Component and it is, in the honest assessment of the people who have needed and utilized it, one of the most under-appreciated and most valuable features of the modern lease-to-own model.

According to the APRO website, a survey of rent-to-own providers found that:

- 97% provide free product service and repairs
- 92% offer loaner products while repairs are completed

Something often called the *Customer Care Component* is a full-service package built into most quality rental-purchase agreements. Maintenance, repairs, proactive checks, replacements when needed, and the genuine assurance that someone has your back the moment something goes wrong. You are never left stranded. You are never handed a broken product and a phone number for a repair service that will charge you separately for the privilege of waiting three weeks for an appointment.

When something fails, and things can fail, it is handled. Promptly. Without additional cost. Without drama.

As mentioned earlier, RNR Tire Express puts it simply: *"Serve, not service."* The distinction is profound. Service is transactional. You pay, we provide, the exchange is complete. Serving is relational. We are invested in your outcome, we show up when you need us, we measure our success by yours.

Their founder Larry Sutton knew the difference firsthand. Before RNR, he had owned franchises in a well-known smoothie brand that shall remain unnamed and found that however good the product, the relationship ended at the counter. A smoothie handed over. A transaction completed. Nothing more. It left him with an unfilled void. He wanted more than that. He wanted to build something where the relationship didn't end at the counter. It began there. That conviction became RNR Tire Express.

The best providers in the lease-to-own industry live that distinction every day. The worst forget it. Knowing the difference before you move forward is one of the most valuable things this book can help you do.

Sheila : Respect She Wasn't Expecting

Sheila wasn't looking for help. She was looking for tires.

The tires on her pickup had been getting worse for months. Every time it rained, she gripped the steering wheel a little tighter. Every time she heard the familiar thump of worn tread rolling over cracked pavement, she told herself she would deal with it next paycheck.

Then the next paycheck came and went.

And then another.

Being a widow had taught her how to stretch a dollar farther than most people thought possible. She worked the dinner shift at a local restaurant, picked up extra hours when she could, and had become an expert at deciding which problem needed solving first. The trouble was that life rarely waited its turn. Tires didn't care what was left in the checking account.

When she finally pulled into the tire store parking lot, she already knew how the conversation was supposed to go. Someone would tell her what she needed. Someone would tell her what it cost. She would smile politely while doing the math in her head and trying not to show how impossible the number felt.

She had lived through that conversation before.

What she wasn't prepared for was Kenny.

He greeted her with the easy confidence of someone who genuinely enjoyed helping people. Not the rehearsed friendliness that disappears the moment a customer says they can't afford something. Real friendliness. The kind that makes you feel welcome before a single word about money is spoken.

As Kenny slowly walked around her truck, Sheila found herself bracing for bad news.

When he returned with the estimate, he sat down beside her and walked through everything line by line. No pressure. No sales pitch. No sighs disguised as patience. No subtle reminder that she wasn't the kind of customer who could simply pull out a credit card and make the problem disappear.

Instead, he explained her options.

When he told her about a payment plan that would let her put down a small amount today and then spread the cost over six months, same as cash, Sheila felt something she hadn't expected to feel that day.

Relief.

Not the dramatic kind. Not tears or celebration. Just the quiet release of a burden she had been carrying for weeks.

For the first time since walking through the door, she stopped calculating. She stopped wondering what bill would have to wait. She stopped rehearsing the apology she had prepared for not being able to afford what she needed.

Kenny never made her feel like a problem that needed solving. He treated her like a human being worthy of being served.

An hour later, Sheila climbed back into her truck on a set of brand-new tires. As she pulled onto the road, the ride felt smoother, but that wasn't what stayed with her. What she remembered was the feeling she carried away from that store.

Respect.

It had been a long time since a business had made her feel that.

Years later, she would still remember Kenny's name. Not because he sold her tires.

Because he saw her.

And sometimes the most valuable thing a business provides isn't the product listed on the invoice. It's the reminder that dignity should never be reserved only for those who can afford to pay all at once.

Sheila didn't receive charity that day. She didn't receive special treatment. She received something far more powerful: a solution that fit her life and a human being who treated her with respect while helping her find it.

That is the difference between providing a service and truly serving someone.

The service was the tires. The serving was everything else.

Sarah : Dead Washer — Dead of Night

Sarah stood in her small Florida laundry room, staring at the washer that had suddenly gone silent mid-spin. Water sloshed inside, and a growing puddle crept across the floor. Her boys were already asleep in the next room, their new school backpacks lined up neatly by the door, empty and waiting for the supplies she still needed to buy before the first bell rang in just a few days.

She felt the familiar wave of exhaustion and panic rise in her chest. She had already stretched every dollar thin for school clothes, shoes that offered a bit of room to grow, and the mountain of supplies on the teacher's list. The thought of dragging baskets of wet laundry to the dingy 24-hour laundromat again, late at night, leaving kids with a sitter she really couldn't afford, put a knot in her stomach.

Then she remembered the person at her rent-to-own store had mentioned they would handle any issues. Trying her best to search her memory, the conversation in her head started up:

Did it cost extra?
It had to cost extra.
There was no way I could have afforded add-ons.
I guess it's worth a shot to call.

She was just so exhausted. So, with hesitant fingers, she dialed the number. She was so worried that it would cost money she just didn't have right now. A calm, kind voice answered. It wasn't Tony, but the person listened patiently as Sarah explained her problem. Then, a smile started to broaden on her face. Now the voice in her head was bouncing with joy and relief:

What?
Someone is coming out tomorrow?
No extra charge?
No claim forms to fill out?

Sarah got the help she needed—quick, professional, and genuinely caring.

The polite young guy arrived on time, fixed the spin cycle with efficient hands, and even wiped up the remaining water so Sarah wouldn't have to. That afternoon, the washer was humming again, clothes tumbling cleanly, and she stood in her kitchen folding school shirts with an ocean of relief pouring over her.

In a world that often asks single mothers to be superhuman, the simple act of reliable support gave her breathing room. It let her focus on what mattered most: being present for her children as they started a new school year, smiling as they showed off their freshly washed favorite shirts.

Sarah's a great mom and the true steadiness of her family's story—doing her best every single day, and now knowing she has a trusted partner when life throws an unexpected curve.

Robert : Not Left to Figure It Out Alone

Robert had always thought of himself as a capable man in many ways. For the last forty-three years he had worked hard, provided for his family, and faced life's challenges with steady strength. But after his beloved wife Margaret passed away, the house felt different. Too quiet, too full of small decisions he had never needed to make alone.

Margaret had been the heart of their home. She handled the repairs, the calls to service people, the little things that kept their daily life running smoothly. Robert had never been what one would call "handy." Now, here he was at seventy-one and on a tight fixed income, staring at a leaning sofa with its leg protruding out at an angle that it shouldn't be. He got down on the floor and looked under it wondering what he should do.

He ran a hand over the cushion on that side where Margaret loved to sit and so many memories of evenings spent watching their favorite shows together started flooding back.

Margaret had chosen the living room set when they visited a local rent-to-own when they were downsizing their lives for retirement. He remembered her saying, "It's just the perfect color. It reminds me of the suit you wore at our wedding." She loved that sofa. Hesitantly, he picked up the phone and called the store, not sure what to expect.

Not very long after, there was a knock at the door. Robert was met by a smiling faced young man. “Hi, Mr. Reed. I’m Teddy. Do you remember me from when we delivered your furniture last year?” With a sigh of relief, he said, “Why yes, Teddy. I had forgotten that, but I think I do remember you. So glad to see you again.”

Teddy was patient and respectful. No long explanations. No skeptical questions about whether the issue was really his responsibility. Sooner than Robert had expected, Teddy explained that the sofa leg only needed a bolt. He had tightened it and the sofa was back to good-as-new. The whole process was handled with such kindness and efficiency that he felt a surprising wave of emotion as he watched Teddy drive away.

“Wow. That young man made it look easy and had it handled in no time,” he said, his voice thick with feeling. “No questions. No hassle. It gave me peace I didn’t know I needed. I wasn’t left figuring it out alone.”

In the weeks that followed, Robert sat on that repaired sofa with a cup of coffee each morning, looking out the window at the bird feeder Margaret had loved. The small act of reliable support reminded him that he didn’t have to carry every burden by himself anymore. It gave him space to grieve, to remember the good years, and to slowly rebuild a new rhythm for his future days.

Robert is the secret hero of his life's later chapters. He is still strong, still enjoying his life, still learning how to navigate without his partner. The rent-to-own company's commitment to standing by its customers didn't just fix a sofa. It gave a grieving widower a little more peace, a little more dignity, and the comforting knowledge that even in his loneliest season, someone had his back.

Later, when Robert contacted the store to let them know he was going to take ownership of his sofa and end his rental-purchase agreement. They told him the amount he needed to do that. The next week, he called the store again, just to thank them once more. "You didn't just get me furniture," Robert said. "You let me keep a piece of my life with me."

What These Stories Have in Common

None of these families were irresponsible. None of them were financially reckless. They were looking for a fair chance. None of them deserved the barriers that traditional credit systems placed in their path. They were trying to keep moving forward, raising kids, honoring memories, staying safe on the road, giving the next generation a solid start.

They were productive people, employed, contributing, trying, who may have needed access to essential goods at moments when the conventional financial system offered them nothing. Or they may have just found the perfect item for their home and wanted to keep their limited nest-egg safe for a future need.

And in each case, the rent-to-own model didn't just provide a product. It provided a dignified yes at the exact moment it was needed most.

These aren't dramatic Hollywood moments. They're small, everyday victories happening in towns and cities across the country right now

RTO offered them a solution. A genuine one. Immediate. Dignified. And they built lives around it. Many may find that to be an excellent choice. Some may even say it was their best decision.

They remind us that access done right isn't about luxury. It's about meeting people exactly where they are with respect, practicality, and the simple power of saying yes when it matters.

Most anyone would agree. That's a better system.

* * *

Chapter 9

How a Generation Rewrote the Rules

The last twenty-five years have tested American families like few other periods in modern history.

The 2008 financial crisis, the COVID-19 pandemic, persistent inflation that ate away at paychecks, and job markets that shifted faster than most could keep up. Each shock delivered the same clear lesson: tying up too much of your money in the things you own can become a serious risk.

When life throws an unexpected curveball, like a job loss, a big medical bill, or a family emergency, assets tied up in furniture, appliances, or other stuff suddenly feel out of reach. Families who kept their options open fared better. Those who stretched to buy more often found themselves stuck, struggling to sell things quickly or pause payments they could no longer afford.

This isn't a criticism of ownership itself. It's simply the hard reality that millions of people lived through.

Resilience Against the Unexpected

Rent-to-own was designed exactly for this kind of unpredictable life. It offers manageable payments, the freedom to return an item and walk away if things change, and the choice of keeping more cash available when it matters most.

Far from being a compromise, this way of accessing things has proven to be a smarter, more resilient path through the storms that every life eventually brings.

Younger Americans picked up these lessons naturally. Many watched their parents struggle through 2008 and grew up in an economy built on streaming music, subscribing to software, and upgrading devices the moment something newer made sense. To these smart cookies, access isn't settling. It's the practical choice that keeps life flexible. They see traditional ownership as the thing that ties you down.

The rest of the market is finally catching up to this way of thinking, but the rent-to-own industry has been living it for decades, long before anyone started calling it the "access economy."

Millions of families, especially in rural areas, never expected to find themselves abandoned by traditional banking. They live in banking deserts with no branch within ten miles. They can't always wait for traditional credit approvals when life throws an unexpected curveball. They need a working refrigerator, safe tires, or a laptop for school right now. For many, the local rent-to-own store that's been on Main Street for thirty years is the most reliable, and sometimes the only, place that says yes. Its importance to these communities keeps growing.

Keeping Pace with Rapid Change

This shift matters even more as everything speeds up. The television you buy today may be outdated in eighteen months. The laptop you invest in can feel slow in three years. With artificial intelligence changing what every device can do, obsolescence isn't occasional anymore. It's constant.

Families who own their technology end up absorbing every wave of upgrades and lost value. Families who choose access stay current, stay flexible, and never find themselves paying for yesterday's best.

Here's something a lot of people don't realize: there's a real environmental upside too.

Americans toss out more than 12 million tons of furniture and household items every year. According to the United Nations, electronic waste, already one of the fastest-growing waste streams, is on track to reach 82 million tons worldwide by 2030. Every appliance that ends up in a landfill, every television replaced and thrown away, carries a hidden cost.

Rent-to-own has been working on the same idea that people now call the circular economy for decades: products get maintained, repaired, returned, refurbished, and put back into use instead of just getting tossed. The industry was doing this long before it had a trendy name.

The Digital Shift

One of the biggest recent changes in the lease-to-own world didn't happen inside traditional RTO stores. It happened inside the stores most Americans already shop in every week.

Virtual Rent-to-Own (VRTO) lets regular retailers offer lease-to-own options right at the checkout counter as an alternative to credit cards or traditional financing.

For the customer standing at the counter, it means access is no longer limited to what a dedicated rent-to-own store may offer. You can now get lease-to-own terms on a much wider range of products without credit needed, without taking on debt, and with the same easy exit options that have always been part of the model.

Something interesting is happening in the rent-to-own world right now. A healthy tension the smartest operators are thinking about.

On one side are the big digital platforms: Acima, Progressive Leasing and others. They bring speed, scale, and the ability to offer lease-to-own at checkout in thousands of stores with approvals in seconds. They reach customers the old storefront model never could.

On the other side is the local rent-to-own store, the independently owned shop on Main Street in a small town in rural Missouri, the hills of Appalachia, or the brush country of South Texas. The place where the owner knows your name, knows when payday hits, and has been helping the same families for decades.

The digital platforms can do things at scale that no local store can match. But they can't replace the one thing the local store offers every day: a warm smile, a friendly face, and someone who listens when you speak.

The future isn't choosing between them. It's both. Serving the same families through different doors, in ways that only grow stronger together.

RNR Tire Express built a paperless point-of-sale system not to replace the person behind the counter but to make the experience faster, cleaner, and more dignified.

Aaron's and Rent-A-Center have invested in digital tools while keeping their doors open in the rural communities that count on them. APRO is building standards that help both sides grow.

The revolution didn't end. It just got an upgrade. And it's still picking up speed.

It's Nothing New for the Coming Gens

There is a generation coming of age right now, the youngest edge of Gen Z and the Gen Alpha kids right behind them, for whom none of this feels new. It's simply the only world they've ever known.

They've never owned a music collection. Never bought a movie. Never purchased software. They just subscribe. They grew up in a world where asking "do you own it?" sounds a little odd. The only question that makes sense is "can you get to it when you need it?"

For this generation, rent-to-own needs no explanation. No credit required, flexible payments, the freedom to walk away, someone who shows up when something breaks, and same-day delivery when the need is real. They'll look at it and simply say: yeah, that makes sense

For them, this way of living isn't something to adopt. It's the water they swim in.

This isn't a lifestyle only for high-income executives. It works for real families in all kinds of situations. The ALICE family that needs a reliable refrigerator today, the young couple furnishing their first home while keeping savings untouched, the retired teacher leasing a mobility scooter because she refuses to slow down, and the rural family whose local rent-to-own store has been part of their community longer than some of their kids have been alive.

All of them are living some version of the same truth.

It was never about owning the title or holding the deed. It was always about a home well furnished, a life fully lived, and the freedom to upgrade whenever something better came along.

That kind of life isn't some far-off dream. It's waiting for you in the store down the street — the one that's been saying yes with a smile for thirty years or more.

* * *

Chapter 10

Three Boxes, One Teal Couch, and a Fresh Start

When Cindy left, she took three boxes.

One held clothes for herself and Becca. Another held photographs, paperwork, and the things you grab when your whole life suddenly needs to fit inside a car. The third box carried the pieces of herself that existed before the relationship and that, she had decided, would exist after it too: a ceramic bowl her mother gave her when she moved into her first grown-up place with a roommate at nineteen, two chipped coffee mugs she refused to throw away, and a stack of birthday cards she had saved for reasons she couldn't fully explain.

Her mother used to buy her clothes in the same blue-green shade when she was little. Not blue exactly. Not green either. A color somewhere in between that her mother always called teal. Cindy wore a teal dress in her second-grade school picture and insisted on wearing it so often that the elbows faded before she outgrew it.

She left everything else.

Not because she had to. Because she wanted to. Because starting over meant starting clean, and clean meant not dragging pieces of the old life into the new one. The couch could stay. The dishes could stay. The bed they had shared for four years could absolutely stay. Cindy had spent enough time carrying things that didn't belong to her. She wasn't carrying them anymore.

She loaded the boxes into her little SUV while Becca held a stuffed rabbit under one arm and asked whether they would still watch cartoons on Saturday mornings. Cindy told her yes because some promises are too important to leave uncertain. Then she buckled her daughter into the back seat, started the engine, and drove away without looking in the rearview mirror once.

That was a Tuesday.

By the following Monday, she had signed a lease on a small two-bedroom place across town. It was clean, safe, and completely empty except for the air mattress her sister loaned her and the smell of fresh paint that still lingered near the baseboards. When sound bounced off empty walls, homes always seemed larger than they really were. This one sounded enormous.

Cindy

Cindy, at thirty-four, was learning how to begin again.

The shame came first because it usually does. The voice that asks whether you should have seen the ending sooner. Whether you stayed too long. Whether stronger people would have somehow arranged life differently so they wouldn't be standing barefoot in an empty place while their seven-year-old asked where the couch was going to go.

Cindy knew that voice well. She argued with it during long showers and while unloading groceries and once at two in the morning while sitting cross-legged on the floor eating dry cereal from a paper bowl because she still didn't have kitchen chairs.

But Cindy had another voice too, and over time it became louder.

Cindy had always been easy to love. She owned too many colorful coffee mugs and could never pass the clearance rack at garden centers without trying to rescue dying plants she insisted only needed encouragement. She decorated for holidays with a level of enthusiasm that embarrassed Becca slightly and delighted neighborhood children enormously. She named her cars. Her first car had been named

Roxy for reasons nobody, including Cindy, fully understood.

She also volunteered twice a month at the nursing home near her office. Not because she had extra time—nobody raising a child alone has extra time—but because loneliness bothered her. She painted nails, played cards, and listened to stories she had already heard three or four times because the residents deserved someone willing to hear them again.

"You remind me of my daughter," people there often told her.

Cindy's heart would clinch just a bit. She would look up with her eyes going damp each time she was told that. She had lost her own mother at twenty-six. Maybe grief had simply taught her to notice lonely people.

Somewhere in those first days after moving, Cindy made a decision. Starting over wasn't punishment. Starting over was proof she had finally stopped pretending everything was okay when it wasn't.

That part had taken courage.

Everything after that was just getting things done.

Becca needed a bed. They needed somewhere to sit and watch movies, and slowly build routines strong enough to make empty rooms stop echoing.

Money was tight. Separation had taken care of that. The separation had done a number on her credit too. Joint accounts closed badly. A few payments missed during the worst of it. Nothing she was ashamed of, but enough to make a credit application feel like one more door that might say no.

What Cindy had was a steady paycheck every two weeks, a job she was good at, and absolute refusal to let empty rooms become the thing that finally defeated her after everything else she had already survived.

A coworker mentioned lease-to-own during lunch one day while stealing fries off Cindy's plate.

"I used it after my divorce," she said casually. "Nobody made it weird."

That mattered more than Cindy expected.

Building It Back

The store was nothing like she expected.

She had braced herself without realizing she was bracing herself. Some leftover muscle memory from years of navigating systems that made you feel small before they decided whether to help you. She walked in with her chin up, her answers ready, and her guard just slightly raised.

Nobody asked for her credit score. Nobody made a face at her situation. The woman who helped her asked what she needed and listened while Cindy described it, walking her through the options without a single moment that felt like judgment.

Cindy stood by until a twin bed had been selected. Becca chose it after serious deliberation.

Then came the couch.

A couch in deep teal—the same blue-green shade her mother used to call 'her color.' Cindy had wanted furniture in that color for years but had always heard opinions about practicality and what colors adults were supposed to choose. Standing in the showroom, she pointed to the teal couch without asking anyone else what they thought.

The weekly payment fit her budget. The documents she signed were clear. If anything broke, the store handled the repair. If her situation changed, she could return any item and walk away from the lease account without the decision following her anywhere.

The couch and bed arrived on a Saturday morning. Becca supervised the placement of her bed and the new couch with the authority of someone who had strong feelings about which wall it should be placed on. She had once read a book about Feng Shui and now considered herself something of an expert.

Cindy glammed up the couch with two throw pillows she bought at a discount store, in exactly the colors she wanted, and stood back to look at it for a long moment.

Then she realized that nobody was standing over her shoulder telling her it was the wrong color.

That thought made her laugh, standing alone in her living room on a Saturday afternoon.

Becca wandered in and asked what was funny.

Cindy just grinned.

Becca looked at the couch, then at her mother, decided adults were strange creatures, and went back to her room.

Six Months Later

Cindy says the first few months were survival.

By the end of the first year, she had started to live again.

The job got better. A promotion she had been passed over for twice finally came through, and with it a raise that changed what the budget looked like at the end of every month. Becca settled into school, found her people, and stopped asking questions about the old place that Cindy never quite knew how to answer.

Somewhere in the middle of that first year, Cindy looked around their home and took stock.

The couch had earned its place.

That ridiculous, wonderful teal still made her smile every morning. Sometimes sunlight from the window caught the fabric just right and reminded her of the dress her mother used to call her lucky color.

Becca's twin bed had suddenly been outgrown. Becca herself was taller now and had developed strong opinions about almost everything, including furniture.

Cindy called the store.

She bought out the lease contract on that fabulous teal couch. It were staying. It had become part of what their home was now.

She returned Becca's little twin bed. No drama. No penalty. Just a phone call and a pickup, followed by another trip to the store where Becca spent forty-five minutes choosing a new bed with the same serious authority she had brought to the first one, but this time if was a full-size bed. She had said, *I'm bigger and I deserve a bigger bed, especially if I want to have sleepovers.*

She set up a new lease account for Becca's bed selection.

Standing in the store that second time felt different from the first. Originally, she had walked in with her guard up and her chin out and her answers ready. This time she walked in knowing exactly how everything worked, knowing she would be treated fairly, knowing she had options in every direction.

She was comfortable.

She was confident.

She was no longer bracing for impact.

What Cindy Knows About Clean Starts

Leaving with three boxes was the bravest thing Cindy ever did. She will say that plainly if you ask her.

But she will also tell you that the bravery didn't stop there. Starting over in an empty place with a seven-year-old and a budget that didn't have a lot of room required its own kind of courage. The daily kind. The kind that does not get acknowledged because it looks like just getting on with it.

Lease-to-own was part of how she made it through that first transitional year.

Not because it solved everything.

Because it solved the immediate thing.

The empty rooms became a home. Becca had a bed she chose herself. Cindy had a couch in exactly the color she wanted. And those had arrived without anyone making her feel like her situation was a problem they were graciously overlooking.

The access model understood something about Cindy's life that a credit application couldn't have captured. Her situation was temporary. Her income was real. Her ability to manage a weekly payment was solid. None of that showed up in a score. All of it showed up in how she lived her life. After that first year, she had bought out what earned its place and returned what didn't, then she walked out of that store that second time the same way she had driven away from her old life on that Tuesday.

Chin up.

Eyes forward.

Not looking back.

The teal couch stayed.

So did the ceramic bowl.

Some things earn their place by surviving with you.

* * *

Chapter 11

What You Gain by Not Owning

Not everyone reacts the same way when they first hear about choosing access over permanent ownership. Some people light up right away. They feel a sense of relief at the idea of lighter payments, the freedom to adapt when life changes, and the ability to return something that no longer fits their needs. For them, the thought of month-to-month flexibility feels like a breath of fresh air.

You might even recognize this free-spirited side in someone like Holly Holliday, the lively substitute teacher Gwyneth Paltrow played on the TV series *Glee*. Holly lived fully in the temporary. Month-to-month leases, paper plates, and a heart that resisted anything too permanent. She thrived on movement and possibility.

On the other end of the spectrum are those who hold on tightly to everything. Think of Charles Foster

Kane in the classic film *Citizen Kane.* The powerful mogul who spent a lifetime collecting, acquiring, and filling his vast mansion Xanadu with crates of statues, rooms full of objects, and possessions so numerous they were simply warehoused and forgotten.

What started as a desire for significance and security eventually left him surrounded by things and empty of everything else. Ownership without purpose isn't wealth. It's storage. And in the film's final, unforgettable moment, the one thing Kane truly wanted wasn't in any of those warehouses. It was a childhood sled, simple, wooden, long gone.

"*Rosebud.*"

The things we accumulate rarely turn out to be the things that matter.

And it's completely okay. We're all wired a little differently. Some hearts find joy in building deep roots and holding on tight. Others, like Holly, thrive when they can move more freely through the seasons of life without heavy anchors holding them back. The important thing is being honest with yourself about what genuinely helps you and your family feel steady, hopeful, and at peace.

For those who feel that subtle pull toward more breathing room, the ones who smile at the thought of manageable payments and the freedom to adjust when jobs change, kids grow, or surprises arrive, this idea can be genuinely life-giving.

When you choose access over ownership you are not simply avoiding a cost. You are earning something real.

You are earning freedom.

You Gain Freedom to Handle Life's Curveballs

Life has a way of introducing plot twists when you least expect them. A rollercoaster drop you didn't see coming.

One month you're doing fine. The next, the car needs major repairs, the kids need new school clothes, or a medical bill lands in your mailbox.

When most of your money is committed and tied up in things you own, those surprises hit harder. You're stuck trying to sell stuff quickly, often at a loss, or juggling payments you must make but can no longer handle comfortably.

With access, you keep more breathing room. You're not locked into actual long-term debt. If circumstances change, you can return the item and walk away cleanly with no credit damage, no collections, no guilt. Those choices become a welcomed safety net.

You're not giving up comfort. You're protecting your ability to handle whatever comes next without everything falling apart.

You Gain the Ability to Stay Current

Think about how fast things change now.

The laptop you bought two years ago already feels slow. The television that was "top of the line" last year is already being outsold by newer models with better picture and smarter features. When you own these things outright, you're stuck with yesterday's technology while paying for it month after month.

When you choose access, you stay current without the financial penalty. You use what you need while it serves you well. When something meaningfully better arrives, you can upgrade without the headache of selling the old one at a fraction of what you paid. You never own the obsolescence.

It's like upgrading your phone. You get the latest version when it actually improves your life, not when the financing schedule says so.

You Gain the Freedom to Change Your Mind

One of the most valuable gifts of access is the ability to say, "This isn't working for me anymore."

Maybe the elliptical machine looked perfect in the store but now sits untouched in the corner. Maybe the big dining table felt right when you moved in, but your life has shifted and a smaller setup would suit you better. With ownership, you're stuck figuring out how to sell it, store it, or live with the regret.

With access, you simply return it. No guilt. No lengthy sales process. No absorbing the depreciation. You keep what serves you in this season of life and let go of what doesn't.

That freedom to change course without penalty is incredibly liberating once you experience it.

Paul had been dreaming about that big, luxurious massage chair for months. Every time he walked past the showroom, it practically called his name from the window. It had soft leather, gentle curves, promising to melt away the knots in his back after another long, tiring day. He could already picture himself sinking into it each evening, the low hum of vibration working its magic, turning his living room into a personal sanctuary. It felt like the reward he'd earned, the one thing his weary body truly deserved. So he brought it home on a rent-to-own plan, heart full of hope.

That first night, he settled in with a happy sigh. The chair cradled him perfectly. For a shining moment, he felt like he'd just made the smartest decision of his adult life, like he'd finally given himself permission to relax and be taken care of.

But six weeks later, the chair had become something else entirely. It sat silently in the corner of his living room like an elegant, oversized piece of modern art. Beautiful, but strangely out of place. Because Paul discovered something important about himself: he wasn't the "sink in and stay still" kind of guy after all.

His real way of unwinding? Moving. A brisk walk around the neighborhood at dusk, tinkering in the garage with his tools, chasing whatever felt alive and active. The chair's gentle vibrations, which had seemed so inviting in the showroom, now felt almost intrusive, like it was politely asking him to sit down and be still when every part of him wanted to keep going.

The version of Paul who had fallen in love with the chair in the bright lights of the store turned out to be a completely different person from the homebody who lived in his house.

So he took a deep breath, picked up the phone, called the store, and scheduled a pickup. No drama. No second-guessing. He returned the chair with a light heart and zero guilt. Just the small cost of six weeks' payments and the gentle, satisfying realization that he now knew himself a little better than before.

There was no stale listing lingering on Facebook Marketplace. No awkward garage-sale haggling. No surprise storage fees piling up. Just a clean, graceful exit from something that hadn't quite fit.

If he had bought it outright, he would have been stuck with the full price and the real weight of living every day with a mistake that was hard to undo. But because he had chosen access instead of ownership, he walked away lighter. He got to test the dream, learn the truth about himself, and move forward without punishment.

In the end, the real gift wasn't the chair. It was the freedom to be wrong for a little while, yet still come out ahead.

You Gain Time and Peace of Mind

Ownership often comes with a hidden load of invisible chores. You become responsible for maintaining the item, handling repairs, worrying about breakdowns, tracking its depreciation, and eventually figuring out how to sell or dispose of it when the time comes. All of these tasks consistently consume your time, attention, and mental energy. Energy that could otherwise be spent enjoying time with your family, advancing your career, pursuing your hobbies, or simply resting and recharging.

When you choose access instead of ownership through rent-to-own, many of those burdens simply lift away. Maintenance and service are typically handled for you. The constant worry about market value, unexpected repairs, or resale complications disappears. Instead of managing the item, you get to truly live with it. Using it freely without the weight of long-term responsibility.

That freed-up time and peace of mind add up in meaningful ways. They create more room for the things that matter most: deeper connections with loved ones, greater focus at work, more energy for passions, and the simple relief of having one less thing to worry about.

What You Don't Lose

Here's the part that surprises many people: choosing access doesn't mean giving up quality or pride in your home.

You can still have nice furniture, reliable appliances, safe tires, and current technology. You just get them on terms that fit your real life instead of forcing your life to fit the old ownership model.

You still get to enjoy the things that improve your days. The couch where your family gathers, the appliances that help keep your groceries fresh and family meals prepared, the tires that get you safely to work.

You just carry less weight while doing it.

Those Next Chapters of Life

Perhaps the most under-appreciated part of choosing flexibility is what happens when life changes. And life always changes.

The young professional who, two years ago, furnished a spacious condo rental when times were good, suddenly finds herself needing to relocate for a better opportunity. She then discovers that moving owned furniture across the country costs more than the furniture is even worth.

The couple who raised children in a large family home find themselves, twenty years later, rattling around in rooms they no longer need, met with the realization that unwinding decades of accumulated assets takes months, costs thousands of dollars, and extracts an emotional toll nobody warned them about.

Consider this: The Los Angeles Times, citing consumer research on household accumulation, reported that the average American home contains more than 300,000 items. As we mentioned in Chapter 3, the storage industry, which exists almost entirely to house the overflow of American accumulation, generates more than $45-$48 billion annually.

To put this in perspective: Americans collectively pay more each month to store their possessions than they spend on their cell phone bills, their full-coverage car insurance, or their daily coffee runs. More than streaming subscriptions and gym memberships combined. For many households, the monthly storage bill rivals what they spend on food takeout and delivery. They are paying, month after month, to stockpile things they don't use — and calling it a necessity.

The lease-to-own model offers a direct response to this particular irony. A portable storage building delivered to your property through a lease-to-own program costs, in monthly payments, roughly what many households are already spending on an off-site storage unit. Except that the building is on your land, accessible on your schedule, and comes with a path to ownership at the end of the term. The access model does not just offer an alternative to the storage problem. In this category, it secretly solves it.

That is not accumulation serving people. That is people serving accumulation.

The person choosing lease-to-own faces a fundamentally different transition. They have less to unwind and fewer assets to dispose of. They will have a bit more freedom to move toward their next chapter without prior possessions demanding attention and resolution.

Flexibility and Real-Life Strength

True strength with money isn't about collecting the biggest pile of stuff or owning everything outright. It's about being able to face the hard days life throws at you and still keep moving forward, with your head held high and your options open.

Think about it this way. When you pour most of your hard-earned money into owning lots of things, that money gets locked away inside couches, appliances, and electronics. If something unexpected happens, like a sudden car repair, a medical bill, a flooded basement, or even something wonderful like a better job that requires a move, it can be surprisingly hard to get that money back out when you need it most. You can end up feeling trapped by the very things you bought hoping they would make life better.

For the millions of Americans who have navigated job losses, medical crises, and economic disruptions over the past two decades, the difference between a flexible financial life and a rigid one was often the difference between a difficult period and a genuinely devastating one.

The Rent-to-Own Difference

Payments you can actually manage week by week or month by month. You're not tying up a large chunk of money all at once. And because you have the freedom to return an item if your circumstances change, you keep real breathing room in your budget, the kind that means when life gets tough or a new door opens, you're not stuck. You have choices. Room to breathe. The ability to adjust without everything falling apart.

This way of living is not just about convenience or lifestyle preference. At its most fundamental level, it is about the capacity to weather the storms that every life contains, and to emerge from them with options still intact and a future still open.

Counting What Counts

The financial world is quick to add up what flexible options might cost you on paper. But it's much slower to measure what those choices to adapt are truly worth to your peace of mind, your family's stability, and your freedom to simply live fully in the present.

When you step back and look at the full picture, honestly weighing the hidden costs of traditional ownership against the real, personal value of being able to adapt, the math often tells a different story than the old conventional wisdom suggests.

The smart choice isn't the same for everyone, and this book has never pretended otherwise. Sometimes ownership is absolutely the right tool and no honest guide would argue differently. But for many of us, the value of that choice is real, substantial, and compounding.

By choosing access and flexibility, you're not making a compromise. You're making a wise investment in freedom and in the beautiful ability to shape your life around who you are today, right now, and through every season still ahead.

You deserve tools that serve you, not the other way around.

That is choosing, deliberately and wisely, to thrive.

* * *

Chapter 12

How Alice Let Ray
Think It Was His Idea

Ray was the kind of man who fixed things. Not just around the house, though he certainly did that too. He fixed problems. If the sink leaked, Ray had tools out before most people finished describing the issue. If neighbors needed help moving furniture or jump-starting a truck battery, Ray was already walking across the yard before they finished asking.

People depended on men like Ray because men like Ray rarely complained.

That had been true since he was young.

His father had worked maintenance at a textile mill and believed strongly in two things: showing up and pushing through. Ray grew up hearing the same phrases over and over.

"If it hurts, keep moving."

"Rest later."

"Things don't fix themselves."

Those lessons served him well for most of his life.

What they didn't teach him was how to recognize when he was the thing that needed fixing.

Ray would replace a water heater without hesitation. He would buy new tires for Alice's car before she noticed the tread wearing thin. He kept the truck serviced, the gutters clean, and the fence standing straight after storms rolled through.

What Ray didn't spend money on was himself.

Comfort felt unnecessary.

Necessary things made sense to him.

Comfort felt optional.

Alice understood this because she had spent twenty-three years married to him.

The mattress had been with them for twelve of those years.

Ray never considered the mattress part of the problem. In his mind, it was still doing what mattresses do. The fact that it leaned slightly toward his side now, that the center dipped enough to make rolling over an event instead of a movement, that the springs had long ago lost whatever fight springs are supposed to win—none of that registered.

His back hurt.

That was the problem.

The ache lived low across his spine and settled deepest in the mornings. By afternoon it usually softened into something manageable. By evening it returned, heavy and familiar.

He mentioned it to his doctor once.

Stretch more.

Lose a little weight.

Physical therapy if it gets worse.

Ray stretched for a few weeks.

Life got busy.

The pain stayed.

Over time he adjusted around it. He lowered himself carefully into chairs. Started staying up later because lying down hurt in a particular way that took time to settle. Began waking early because staying in bed too long stopped feeling restful and started feeling like punishment.

Alice watched all of it.

She noticed the small things first.

The extra seconds before he stood up.

The hand pressed continuously against his lower back when he thought nobody was looking.

How weekend projects slowly disappeared.

How conversations shortened.

Pain takes up space. It moves into places you don't expect. Into patience. Into humor. Into energy. Into the parts of a person that used to belong to everyone else.

Alice knew what the problem was.

She had known for over a year.

The problem was the mattress.

The Conversation

She brought it up on a Saturday morning while sunlight pushed through the kitchen window and Ray sat nursing coffee with both hands, waiting for his back to cooperate with the day.

Alice didn't criticize.

She didn't say, *Your mattress is ruining you.*

She simply mentioned reading about sleep quality and back health and wondered out loud whether it might be worth looking into.

Ray said the mattress was fine.

Alice reminded him it was twelve years old.

Ray argued twelve years wasn't old for a mattress.

Alice gave him the look wives develop after decades of practice—the one that says *I am allowing you the opportunity to arrive at the correct answer yourself.*

Ray drank his coffee.

"A good mattress costs money," he finally said.

There was more behind that hesitation than Ray ever said out loud. Two years earlier, a medical situation had pushed them into bankruptcy. They had come through it and were rebuilding, slowly and steadily the way Ray did everything. But the experience was still fresh enough that walking into a store and filling out a credit application felt like bracing for impact. The high-interest store accounts would still say yes. Ray knew that. But yes from those places had a way of making things worse before they made them better.

Alice told him she had already looked into lease-to-own options and the weekly payment was less than what they spent eating out most Fridays.

Ray had answers for almost everything.

Not that.

They went shopping that afternoon at the little rent-to-own on main street. That place had been there for as long as Alice could remember. She had looked in the windows years ago, but had never stepped inside. She thought to herself, *How could I have never known how big this store was inside?*

She not only hoped for the mattress. Alice silently wished for an entire bedroom that felt less like a room they had inherited from younger versions of themselves. There old furniture had survived humidity, moves, children climbing into the bed to snuggle after bad dreams, and decades of just ordinary life.

It looked tired.

If she was honest, so did they.

Ray crossed his arms walking through the store, which Alice recognized immediately as his posture for *interested but unwilling to admit it.*

He sat on one mattress. Then another. Then another.

On the fourth mattress, something changed. Not dramatically. But just enough. He laid down on it. He rolled to one side. Then onto his back again. His shoulders relaxed first. Then his face.

“This one feels different,” he said with a little smile.

Alice pretended this was surprising.

The furniture arrived the following Tuesday.

Ray took over the assembling of the bed frame himself because there had never been another possible outcome. He tightened bolts twice, adjusted corners three times, and stepped back to inspect it from angles nobody else would ever notice.

That night he climbed into bed and lay flat staring at the ceiling. He stayed still for a long time. Not because something hurt.

Because something didn't.

Three Weeks Later

Alice noticed before Ray did.

He moved differently in the mornings. Not carefully. Just normally. She heard him walking through the kitchen before sunrise one morning and realized something strange. The sounds were missing.

No soft groans or sharp exhale when he stood up. No pauses beside the counter.

It took eleven days before Ray mentioned it.

He came inside from the garage one evening wiping grease from his hands and casually announced that his back had been feeling better lately.

Alice kept drying dishes. "That's good," she said. Ray suggested maybe the stretches had finally started working. Alice smiled into the dish towel. Ray recognized the smile immediately.

“Fine,” he said. “Maybe it was the mattress.”

“Maybe so,” Alice answered.

What neither of them said out loud was how much pain had stolen from him. The shorter conversations. The less busy weekends. The tired version of Ray who had slowly disappeared inside discomfort.

Pain rarely stays where it starts. It spreads through a life the way water spreads through wood—slowly enough that you stop noticing until one day everything feels different. The absence of pain works the same way.

Ray slept well that night. And the night after that.

What Ray and Alice Know Now

Several months later, when the budget had breathing room again, they chose to take ownership on their bedroom set.

Ray handled it with one phone call. The way Ray handled most things once he finally decided.

Today he stretches occasionally when he remembers. He gets out of bed without ceremony.

He moves through mornings without negotiating with his back first.

Alice bought a new book for the nightstand on her side of the bed. The table is the right height now. The lamp sits exactly where she wants it. The room finally feels like it belongs equally to both of them.

She started reading again. Ray noticed.

He notices more things now.

* * *

Chapter 13

Taking the Long Way Home

Devon had been driving the same car for three years before anyone noticed it.

Not because the car itself was bad. The car was pretty excellent underneath. A used muscle car with clean lines, a healthy engine, and the kind of bones that people who know cars notice immediately. Devon bought it because it fit his budget and because, standing in a seller's driveway at twenty years old, he could already see what it might become.

For three years he kept it running through equal parts YouTube tutorials, scraped knuckles, and stubbornness. Saturday mornings often found him lying on warm concrete with music playing from his phone speaker while neighbors mowed lawns nearby. He learned which sockets disappeared easiest, which bolts fought back hardest, and how old engines have personalities if you spend enough time with them.

He loved that car.

The problem was the wheels.

The stock set had never matched what he saw in his head. They looked tired. Practical. Like transportation. Every time he walked away from the car in a parking lot, he glanced back and saw potential instead of completion.

For three years, though, potential had to wait.

When you are young and building a life from scratch, there is always something more important. Rent comes first. Insurance comes first. Groceries come first. The tires stay stock because adulthood keeps sending invoices.

Then Devon got the job.

Where Dreams Meet Payday

The job mattered because it was real.

Not temporary. Not seasonal. Not one of those positions where everyone pretended nobody knew how long it would last.

Real salary.

Real benefits.

Real direct deposits.

Devon had worked for it too. For nearly two years he bounced between jobs that paid bills but never quite matched what he knew he could do. He took shifts nobody wanted, showed up early because reliability costs nothing, and secretly watched for opportunities the way shy people often do. Devon wasn't loud. He wasn't naturally the center of attention. In groups, his friends usually filled silences before he did.

Cars were easier.

Cars made sense.

People sometimes didn't.

His first paycheck landed on a Friday afternoon while he was sitting in his car during lunch. He opened his banking app twice because seeing the number once didn't quite feel real. There were responsible plans already waiting for that money. His mother had opinions about savings. His older brother had opinions about emergency funds. Devon mostly agreed with all of them.

Still, after the responsible money had places to go, there was something left.

Not a huge amount.

Just enough.

For months he had been researching wheels the same way he researched everything important. Videos. Forums. Comparison photos. Tire sizes. Offsets. Screenshots saved in folders he pretended were temporary. He knew the weekly payments. He knew the finishes. He knew exactly what fit his car.

He had looked into buying the wheels outright. The math never worked. A quality set installed ran more than his credit card limit could cover, and he wasn't about to blow past that ceiling two months into a job he wanted to keep. Carrying a maxed card into a new chapter felt like the wrong move. He had heard from the older guys at previous jobs about how they were still paying off charges from years back, the interest eating up whatever ground they thought they had made.

He wasn't doing that.

That Friday after work, he drove to the store.

The First Set

Devon was not impulsive.

He asked questions because he always asked questions. He understood the lease-purchase agreement before signing anything. Weekly payments. His freedom to choose to acquire ownership at any time. Return options if life changed. The details mattered because Devon had spent too much of life feeling like everyone else somehow received instructions he missed.

He chose chrome wheels that looked aggressive without trying too hard. The kind that respected the car instead of overwhelming it. Devon had always believed modifications should look like they belonged there.

Installation took a couple of hours.

Long enough for excitement to slowly turn into nervousness.

When they lowered the car back onto the pavement, something happened.

The car looked finished.

Not new.

Not expensive.

Finished.

Driving away felt different even though mechanically nothing changed. The steering felt familiar. The engine sounded the same. But Devon caught reflections in storefront windows and kept smiling without meaning to.

He took the long way home.

Then a longer way.

That evening his phone started buzzing. A friend spotted the car at a gas station. Another wanted pictures. On Monday morning, two coworkers stopped him in the parking lot before he even made it inside.

For three years, people barely noticed the car.

One set of wheels changed that.

What Changed

Devon would tell you the wheels changed the car.

That part is true.

But the bigger change happened somewhere else.

There is something powerful about feeling seen when you have spent years blending into backgrounds. Devon had always been the silent guy. The dependable friend. The one people liked but sometimes overlooked. The wheels gave strangers permission to start conversations, but what surprised Devon was what happened after that.

People stayed.

Car meets stopped feeling intimidating. Conversations became easier when everyone already had something to talk about. Older guys taught him things about his platform he had spent years trying to learn online. His group of friends grew wider. Girls looked twice sometimes.

His guy friends definitely noticed.

There is a particular feeling young men rarely admit wanting. You want your friends to think you are doing well. You want people to notice when your hard work finally starts showing. You want somebody to look at something you built and say, *man, that's nice.*

Devon liked hearing that.

His mother noticed changes too.

Not the wheels specifically.

Just him.

One evening she told him he seemed happier lately while handing him leftovers to take home.

Devon thought about that afterward.

He had always been himself.

Now other people seemed to notice.

The Upgrade

About eight months later, Devon saw another set.

Deeper dish. Better finish. More aggressive stance.

He tried ignoring them.

That lasted about three weeks.

He called the store expecting complicated answers and discovered upgrading was surprisingly straightforward. The remaining value from his current rental-purchase agreement applied toward the new setup. The weekly payment moved up slightly but stayed manageable.

Two hours after arriving on a Saturday morning, he walked back outside.

The first set had transformed the car.

The second set transformed him.

He stood staring at the reflection in the shop window longer than he wanted to admit. Sunlight caught the polished finish. The stance looked perfect.

His phone started buzzing before he reached the first red light.

Again.

What Devon Knows About Upgrades

Devon is twenty-three and has already learned something older people sometimes forget.

You don't always become a new person overnight.

Sometimes you slowly become more visible versions of who you already were.

Lease-to-own worked for Devon because his life was still changing. His income changed. His taste changed. His confidence changed. The first good decision didn't have to become the final decision.

He didn't have to wait years to stop driving the version of the car he had outgrown in his head.

He started where he was.

Then improved from there.

The car still has the same engine. Same body. Same bones. It is still the car Devon bought because the numbers made sense for a young guy trying to get started.

But people notice now.

Devon notices too.

And if you ask his friends, they will tell you he still takes the long way home.

* * *

Chapter 14

The Cost of Ownership

The purchase price is only the beginning of the ownership story and frequently the most flattering part.

Consider the washing machine. You buy it. You install it. You run it for a few years and then, right around the time the warranty expires, as if by design, something fails. Not the motor. Not the tub. The electronics panel. The circuit board that costs $40 to manufacture and, based on real consumer experience, can run $450 or more to replace.

And here is where planned obsolescence shows up uninvited. That hidden, deliberate engineering choice, built into products by design, that has made modern appliances considerably less durable than their forerunners. Forty years ago, your grandmother's washing machine kept spinning dependably for twenty years or more. Today you'll be lucky if yours makes it for seven.

The electronics that run these machines were not designed with longevity in mind. They were designed with replacement cycles in mind. That is not wear and tear. That is a business model. One in which you absorb the full cost.

And here is the part of that method of ownership that almost nobody talks about honestly. Most middle- and lower-income households are not paying cash when they buy these items. They are charging them on credit cards.

According to data from the Consumer Financial Protection Bureau (CFPB), Americans recently paid $160 billion in annual credit card interest. That's billion with a 'B'. The annual interest rate, also know as annual percentage rate (APR), for general-purpose bank credit cards averaged over 25 percent. And for cards that retailers actively encourage at the point of purchase, the rate was over 31 percent. They said these rates are the highest reported in more than 10 years.

4 in 5 American carry an average of four active credit cards making it the mainstream financial tool that most Americans reach for at the point of purchase.

But look at what card usage actually costs where most American already shop:

- Home Depot — 17.99% to 29.99%
- Best Buy — 27.74% to 30.74%
- Rooms To Go — 29.99% to 34.99%

These are not fringe lenders. These are the stores on every major retail strip in America.

Now consider a real example. You purchase a sofa and chair, or a couple of major appliances, for $2,500 using a store credit card. Being generous, let's apply a rate of 25 percent. You receive your monthly statement. You pay the minimum required.

Under the Credit Card Accountability Responsibility and Disclosure Act — the CARD Act — credit card issuers are legally required to disclose on every billing statement exactly what minimum payments will cost you over time. Here is what that disclosure would tell you on a $2,500 balance at 25 percent:

- Original purchase — $2,500
- Total interest charged — $4,072
- Total of payments — $6,572

One in five Americans would pay 2.63 times the original price by making those minimum payments.

To make the comparison concrete, here is what the same $2,500 sofa or appliance set would look like under three common paths (using real interest rate averages):

- **Cash purchase:** $2,500 total.
- **Rent-to-own:** $3,900–$4,700 total paid including service plan [typical weekly payments, kept for full term and not using early ownership options.]
- **Store credit card:** $6,572 total [if minimum payments made.]

If you don't take an early ownership option (although most RTO users do) and you keep the item for the full term, rent-to-own costs more than cash. The difference is the built-in flexibility, free repairs, and the ability to return the item at any time without further obligation.

A really important fact to know: those 1 in 5 cardholders that make only the minimum payment requested will likely have their debt remaining long after the product purchased wears out.

Then there is another 1 in 5 American adults who either don't have access to credit cards at all or choose not to have them.

Remember, unlike lease-to-own, you cannot stop a

credit card statement from following you until the balance is totally paid.

Make these calculations part of your decision when you have a credit card in your pocket to toss on the counter.

Before we go further, the most important question in this entire chapter deserves to be asked plainly. It regards whether it is a good idea to consider utilizing rent-to-own. That question is:

> Compared to what?

To be fair: not every consumer faces the same choice. If you have access to a 0% promotional financing offer, a personal loan at a single-digit interest rate, or simply the savings to pay cash within a month or two — those paths will almost certainly cost you less than rent-to-own at full term. This book has never argued differently.

What it argues is that for the specific population RTO was built to serve, the families without established credit, without savings buffers, without access to favorable financing terms, the honest comparison is not between RTO and a low-interest bank loan. It is between RTO and a store credit card charging 29 to 34 percent interest, or between RTO and simply going without. Seen through that lens, the model looks considerably different than its critics have typically acknowledged.

When the Full-Term Cost Matters

If you plan to keep the item for the entire term and can qualify for credit or save the cash price within a few months, rent-to-own will almost always cost more than buying outright. In that case, the full-term cost is a real consideration. The flexibility, the service, and the exit options still have value, but the math would certainly favor ownership.

There is one more thing worth saying about the cost conversation and it comes from a perspective that most financial comparisons never bother to include.

The Value Equation

Mentioned so often in this book, Seth Godin pens one of the longest-running and most prolific personal blogs in existence and is well known for his bestselling book *Purple Cow*. This influential thinker and strategist recently shared his views on a popular podcast, stating that smart choices aren't always about finding the absolute cheapest option. People pay more than the lowest price because, to them, what they're getting is worth it. They see value that isn't always easy to measure. It might be peace of mind, convenience, dignity, or simply the ability to move forward without being weighed down. When you help people get where they want to be, the decision becomes much easier.

That's one reason rent-to-own can make so much sense: it lets you access what serves your life right now, without forcing you into a long-term commitment that may no longer fit six months in the future.

Rent-to-own lives in that space. The families who choose it are typically aware that credit cards and layaway plans are available. They're simply making a deliberate decision that fits their life better. They are often choosing something the alternatives can't offer: immediate possession, no debt obligation, maintenance included, the freedom to return it, and the dignity of a yes when everything else has said no.

That package has value. Real, measurable, life-improving value. And for the people whose lives it has changed, like Caroline's cold milk, Robert's sofa, Calvin's tires, no interest rate calculation has ever come close to capturing what that value was really worth.

Rethinking the Driveway

The rise of ride-sharing platforms, car-sharing services, and subscription-based transportation has subtly dismantled one of the most deeply held assumptions in American consumer life. That a personal vehicle is a necessity rather than a choice.

For millions of urban Americans, it already isn't. The math has shifted. And understanding why requires an honest look at what car ownership can add to its cost beyond the sticker price.

Consider what ownership honestly requires. You need somewhere to put the vehicle, which means either a garage or driveway built into your housing cost, or a monthly parking fee that in urban areas can rival a car payment itself. You pay for insurance every hour of every day, whether the car is moving or sitting idle while you sleep. Most personal vehicles are in motion for less than five percent of their lives. The other ninety-five percent of the time, you are paying to store a depreciating asset that is doing nothing for you.

And then there is everything the purchase price never mentioned. Oil changes, filters, and fluid top-ups that arrive on a schedule whether you are ready for them or not. Tires that wear and degrade whether the miles are highway or driveway. Wiper blades, brake pads, belts, and batteries that fail without notice and bill without mercy. Car washes and interior cleanups that are optional right up until they aren't. And beneath all of it, the lurking, ever-present possibility of a serious mechanical failure, like a transmission, an engine, a timing chain, that arrives as a single invoice larger than some people's monthly rent.

None of this appears in the monthly payment. All of it arrives in the years that follow.

When you eventually sell the vehicle, you absorb the full depreciation, which is a loss that on a typical vehicle over five years can represent tens of thousands of dollars, on top of every maintenance expense that preceded it.

For urban residents, the combined cost of insurance, parking, maintenance, depreciation, and financing almost always exceeds what the same mobility would cost through a combination of ride-sharing, transit, and occasional rental. For suburban and rural residents, the calculation is different, but the principle remains: the vehicle you own is fighting against your financial flexibility every hour it sits still.

Applying the access mindset to transportation is not a sacrifice. For millions of Americans, it is simply the smarter arithmetic.

What This Means in Real Life

Think about what that does to you and your family on the ground where you work, play, sleep and live. That washing machine with the failed electronics panel, the one that cost $800 to buy and $450 or more to repair, was very often charged on a credit card by the very family who could afford it least. At a 25 percent or more APR, making minimum payments, that $800 appliance does not cost $800. It costs considerably more and the buyer is still paying for it long after the machine itself has been replaced.

The skeptics who attempt to calculate effective interest rates on RTO transactions never ask it. They assume the customer had a bank loan available at seven percent. They assume she had savings. They assume she had options. For most RTO customers, those assumptions are wrong. The real comparison is never between lease-to-own and a cheaper alternative. It is between lease-to-own and the only alternatives offered to her.

Lease-to-own is not competing with a perfect cash-purchase world that many consumers inhabit. It is competing with the credit card trap that is already the norm for millions of American households.

When you make that comparison honestly, lease-to-own's predictable weekly or monthly payment, with no compounding interest, no surprise repair bills, and the option to take early ownership that lets you exit cleanly when you are ready, against a credit card purchase at 25 percent or more APR and with minimum payments extending the debt for years beyond the product's useful life, lease-to-own does not look like a compromise.

Knowing the reality should make you stop and consider. You may have been reaching for the credit card simply because it's what everybody has always done. But now you know there's another way. And knowing your options is always a good thing.

You just may find that rent-to-own and living lighter is truly the smarter choice for you. The one that was waiting all along.

* * *

Chapter 15

When Life Doesn't Go According to Plan

Nobody hands you a warning.

One day everything is moving in the right direction. The job is solid. The paycheck is steady. You finally have a place that feels like yours. And then something shifts. The company announces layoffs. A better job shows up in another city. A relationship ends.

Life changed. But everything you signed up for? Of course, those didn't change.

That gap right there, between where your life went and where your commitments are still standing, is what this chapter is about.

Nick

Nick's grandmother had a living room that could hold the whole family.

Her kitchen was barely bigger than a parking space, but twelve people could eat out of that kitchen and nobody went home hungry. The whole house smelled like cornbread and something slow on the stove. In the living room, the men watched the game on furniture that had been in the family so long nobody could remember where most of it came from. The couch had a worn spot on the left armrest from thirty years of Sunday afternoons. The side table wobbled just a little. None of it matched. All of it felt exactly right.

Nick loved that room. Not because of what was in it. Because of what the room said. This is a life somebody built. Piece by piece. Held together with love.

That's what he wanted someday. That feeling. A place that said the same thing about him.

By twenty-eight, he thought he was almost there.

Good job at a company that seemed stable. Real paycheck hitting the bank every two weeks. An great mobile home rental that was just the right size and in a nice little community that he wasn't embarrassed to have people see. He'd spent one long Saturday putting the living room together, start to finish. A couch that didn't sag. A coffee table he'd picked out himself. Curtains his sister Renee helped him hang, because she had been hanging his curtains wrong for him since he was nineteen and she wasn't about to stop now.

When they finished, Renee stepped back and looked at the room. Then she looked at him. Then she reached up and ruffled his hair the way she had done since he was ten years old, which he pretended to hate and didn't.

"All grown up," she said.

He felt that.

His mind drifted to simple things that suddenly felt possible: having the guys over to watch the game, ordering pizza, laughing late into the evening. He thought about Vanessa too. They'd been dating for a few months, and this was the first place he'd had where inviting her over wouldn't come with an apology or an explanation.

That big screen high-definition TV. Not just any TV. It represented his new chapter beginning.

Only three months later his company announced a restructuring.

The job didn't go away. But the feeling of security did. Another three weeks after that, right in the middle of running numbers he had never needed to run before, a recruiter called. Different city. Better title. Bigger paycheck.

Nick told Renee about it that night. She said exactly what he knew she would say.

"Don't you dare say no."

She was right. He knew she was right. He could feel she was right before he even hung up with her.

But when he sat down across from that monster TV and opened his laptop to figure out what saying yes would honestly cost him, the number stopped him cold.

That TV had payments left. The mobile home lease had months left. Every single thing had been set up for a Nick who was staying put. None of it knew his life had changed direction. None of it cared.

He did the math three different times hoping to get a different answer. Same answer every time.

He sat there and thought: I built this whole setup for a version of my life that is no longer there.

The Part Nobody Talks About

Here's what many people get wrong about moments like Nick's.

They look back and say he should've known better. Should've planned more carefully. Should've seen it coming.

Seen *what* coming, exactly?

Nick didn't make bad decisions. He made normal decisions for the life he had at the time. The job looked stable because jobs usually look stable right up until they don't. The city felt like the right city because it *was* the right city—until a better opportunity appeared somewhere else. He couldn't have predicted the restructuring. He couldn't have predicted the recruiter's call. Nobody can. That is not a planning failure. That is simply life.

The problem was never Nick.

The problem was that every commitment he made locked into place the moment he made it. Solid going in, unyielding once it was set. When life changed direction, those commitments refused to bend. And Nick found himself trapped on the wrong side of them.

So he took the job. He sold half his belongings on Facebook for less than he still owed on them. He was, at least, able to sublet the mobile home without too much fanfare. He said goodbye to the little place he had loved, drove away pulling a moving trailer, and watched that home shrink in the rearview mirror.

He made it work. He always did.

But it cost him. Money, yes. Yet far more than dollars, it came with the slow, soul-draining exhaustion of dismantling a life he had only just finished building.

What Would Have Been Different

Think about what Nick's story looks like if the big screen hi-definition TV works differently.

Lease-to-own would have meant Nick had the huge hi-def television he wanted. His home would have felt like the one he imagined. Renee still ruffled his hair. He still texted Vanessa. The guys still came over for the game. All would have happened.

But after that recruiter called, the math would have been different.

With lease-to-own, Nick could have returned that huge television. No buyout number to hit. No debt following him to the new city. He would have paid as he used it, and then the lease-purchase agreement would have ended when he returned the TV. He would have loaded the car, not the trailer. He would still start fresh in the new place, but would have gotten similar or even better electronics that makes sense for his next chapter.

The TV didn't own him in that scenario. The agreement expected nothing from him except the lease payment for the weeks he actually had it in his living room.

That is the whole idea behind lease-to-own. You get what you need right now, for your life right now. And if your life changes, the agreement changes with it. You are not punished for the fact that you couldn't predict the future. Nobody can predict the future. The lease-to-own model was built knowing that.

Ownership says: make a promise about tomorrow based on what you know today.

Lease-to-own says: let's deal with today, and we'll figure out tomorrow when tomorrow gets here.

For a lot of people, in a lot of chapters of life, that second option is not the lesser choice.

That second option is the smart one.

What Nick Knows Now

Nick still has the big TV. He rented a pricey trailer to haul the huge thing very carefully to the new city. Some things you keep because keeping them makes sense. Some things you keep because you feel you have no other choice.

Renee still teases him about renting a trailer to move his giant oversized TV. He just smiles.

What he knows now is simple. Every purchase is a promise. And the question worth asking before you make that promise is not just, can I afford this. The question is, what happens to this promise if my life goes somewhere I am not expecting.

Because life does often go somewhere unexpected. Not sometimes. Pretty much always, sooner or later.

The people who move through those moments the easiest are not the ones who planned the best. They are the ones who left themselves a door.

Lease-to-own is a door.

About six months into the new city, a guy at work named Carter mentioned he was finally moving out of his sister's place into his own apartment. New city for him too. New job. Excited but stretched thin.

Nick recognized every word of it.

He took Carter to lunch for burgers that Friday and told him the whole story. The TV. The trailer. The math he ran three times hoping for a different answer. The particular kind of tired that comes from dismantling a life you just finished building.

Carter listened without saying much.

Then Nick told him about his discovery of lease-to-own. How the agreement works. What walk-away really means. Why the weekly payment is not the consolation prize — it is the intelligent move when your life is still finding its shape.

Carter asked a few questions. Good ones.

Nick answered every one of them.

Walking back to the office, Carter admitted he had always assumed lease-to-own was for people who had no other options.

"I used to think that too," Nick said.

He didn't look at Carter when he said it. His eyes stayed ahead, his voice calm, as though he'd already wrestled with the idea long ago and come out the other side.

Some lessons you learn in a classroom.

Some you learn hauling a giant television across three states in a rented trailer.

Nick knew which kind stuck longer.

* * *

Chapter 16

Four Flights of Stairs and One Epiphany

Jasmine grew up in a family where ownership meant something. Not in a wealthy way, but in the way families pass beliefs down until nobody remembers where they started. Her parents repaired appliances instead of replacing them. Her grandfather kept receipts folded into envelopes long after warranties expired because paperwork, according to him, had saved more money than hard work ever did. Furniture stayed in families for decades, cars stayed until repairs became embarrassing, and nobody ever threw away a perfectly good appliance just because something newer existed.

Because of that, Jasmine grew up hearing the same phrases repeated often enough that they eventually stopped sounding like opinions and started sounding like facts. Renting was throwing money away. Buying quality once saved money later.

Ownership meant adulthood. Ownership meant success. Ownership meant stability.

For most of her life, she never questioned any of it.

At twenty-seven, Jasmine lived in a small townhouse filled with things that reflected exactly who she was. Her couch came from an aunt who had reupholstered it herself one summer while drinking sweet tea and watching crime shows. Her kitchen table belonged to her grandmother first and still carried tiny scratches from cousins doing homework twenty years earlier. Her bookshelves were simple boards and brackets because Jasmine liked furniture that could be disassembled quickly and moved easily.

Furniture, though, was never the thing Jasmine cared much about. Her thing was technology.

She followed product releases the way some people followed football teams. She watched review videos while folding laundry, listened to technology podcasts while grocery shopping, and somehow always knew which processor, graphics card, or television model people should buy before they asked. Friends texted her before buying laptops. Coworkers stopped by her desk asking about phones. She once spent forty minutes explaining monitor refresh rates to a cousin who absolutely didn't need a forty-minute explanation.

Jasmine had been podcasting for almost a year on equipment she had pieced together from secondhand sources. A microphone that did the job if you positioned it exactly right and kept the windows closed. Headphones with a fraying cable she had taped twice. A bare-bulb desk lamp standing in for the ring light she had not yet justified buying. Software she had learned inside out because knowing your tools is the only way to compensate for their limitations.

The podcast was called *Current* and it covered technology, culture, and what Jasmine called the gap between what people think they want and what can really make their lives better. She had started it mostly to organize her own thinking. Then listeners started showing up. Then more. The growth was steady and real and she could see exactly where it was going.

She could also hear exactly what was holding it back.

The sound quality was good enough for where she had been. It wasn't good enough for where she was going.

Research was Jasmine's comfort zone. Overthinking occasionally became a hobby.

The thing that finally made her question ownership happened while helping her friend Bree move on a weekend in August. Bree had been talking about leaving her old place for almost nearly a year. The neighborhood had changed, the commute kept getting longer, and she finally found something newer across town with quieter neighbors and covered parking. Jasmine showed up expecting a few hours of carrying boxes in exchange for pizza and gratitude.

By nine o'clock that morning, she realized she had badly underestimated what she had gotten herself into.

Oh, What We Do for Friends

The bookshelf came first. It was floor-to-ceiling solid wood, beautiful in the way expensive furniture becomes beautiful after surviving enough years that replacing it feels irresponsible. Four people wrestled it halfway down the first flight of stairs before stopping to discuss angles, strategy, and whether anyone had measured doorways beforehand. The sectional came next, oversized and heavy enough that everyone involved stopped to reconsider what counted as friendship.

By noon, heat had settled into the stairwell and stayed there. Sweat trickled down Jasmine's neck, cardboard rubbed raw spots into her palms, and every trip down another flight of stairs made the moving truck somehow seem farther away. What caught her attention most, though, wasn't the furniture.

It was the electronics.

Boxes filled with old gaming systems from previous generations, monitors, cables nobody recognized anymore, and accessories for products Bree no longer even owned. All these items just kept appearing from closets and cabinets. Of course, her giant TV was another whole story.

"Do you even use half this stuff anymore?" Jasmine asked while carrying another box toward the truck.

Bree shrugged and wiped sweat from her forehead. "Not really. But I paid good money for it."

The answer stayed with Jasmine.

She remembered movie nights when that television felt enormous. She remembered Bree researching specifications for weeks before buying it. She remembered the excitement of unpacking it, setting it up, and showing it off. Now it was just another heavy box that needed carrying.

Then she picked up a box that stopped her cold.

Recording equipment. Professional grade. A condenser microphone still in its original foam casing. A compact mixer with more inputs than Bree had ever used. A pop filter, a boom arm, a ring light still folded in its box, and a set of studio headphones that cost more than Jasmine's entire secondhand setup combined.

She looked at Bree.

Bree made a face that mixed guilt and defensiveness in equal measure. She had gone through a phase and Jasmine remembered her mentioning it long ago. Bree had been going to start a podcast. Had done all the research, bought all the gear, recorded exactly one episode that she never published, and had been carrying the equipment through two moves ever since because she kept thinking she might give it another go someday.

Jasmine set the box down carefully.

She wouldn't dare offer to buy the stuff from Bree. She could see from Bree's face that the equipment had become tangled up in something that had nothing to do with podcasting anymore. It was a symbol of something Bree wasn't ready to let go of yet.

But standing there on that landing, Jasmine did the math in her head.

Bree had spent well over a thousand dollars on equipment she used once. It was sitting in a box. It was moving to a third place. And somewhere in that box was a ring light still in its packaging and a microphone that had never once been in front of a voice worth recording.

Jasmine's own podcast had value and content worth recording.

It just didn't have the equipment yet.

They made fourteen trips to the truck. On the last trip, loading the final box of cables and chargers for devices some of which no longer existed, Bree looked at the packed truck and said she couldn't believe how much stuff she had.

Jasmine said nothing.

But she was doing math in her head that had nothing to do with the move.

The Question She Could Not Unask

Driving home that evening with sore shoulders and tiny cardboard cuts across both hands, Jasmine realized she had been thinking about ownership incorrectly. The problem was never whether people could afford things. The problem was that ownership assumes life will stay the same when living itself means constant change.

Technology changed quickly. Jobs changed. Home locations changed. Relationships changed. Yet every purchase somehow arrived with the expectation that it should continue making sense indefinitely.

That night Jasmine opened her laptop and started researching because research was what she always did when something bothered her. One tab turned into six. Six turned into comparison charts, customer reviews, forums, and eventually spreadsheets. Somewhere in the middle of all that reading, she found lease-to-own options for electronics.

That surprised her.

Furniture made sense. Electronics had never occurred to her.

The more she read, though, the more it matched the way she already thought about technology. Use what fits your life now. Keep it if it earns its place. Return it if your needs change. Upgrade when technology changes.

She read through everything twice because Jasmine rarely trusted good ideas immediately.

Current

The following week she dove heavily into lease-to-own options for the first time. Not for a television. For a microphone.

A proper condenser microphone. A compact mixer. Studio headphones without a fraying cable. And a ring light, the real kind, the kind that every serious podcaster seemed to own and that Jasmine had been substituting a bare desk lamp for since episode one.

She set it all up that evening on her desk in the corner of the bedroom she had always thought of as the *Current* corner. When she turned the ring light on for the first time, the whole setup looked like what she had always imagined it could be.

She sat in front of it for a long moment before hitting the 'record' button.

Her next episode sounded different from the first note. Cleaner. Warmer. The kind of sound that tells a listener without saying a word that the person on the other end takes this seriously.

Her followers noticed the difference before she even mentioned it. Comments started coming in within the first week. People asking what microphone she was using. People saying something had shifted. People sharing the episode because the sound quality finally matched the content quality that had always been there.

Jasmine read every comment.

She had always known where *Current* was going. Now the equipment knew it too.

The gaming console and the television followed the same approach in the months after. Use it. Enjoy it. Buy out early when the item was a keeper and numbers made sense. Return it and upgrade when something better arrived. The decision was always hers, based on what she sincerely wanted, not what she had already spent.

Her little townhouse still had the aunt's reupholstered couch and the grandmother's table with the homework scratches. She wasn't particular about furniture. But her electronics were always up to date and her podcast equipment always matched where *Current* was going, never where it had been.

About six months after that exhausting day of moving, Bree came over and looked around Jasmine's townhouse.

"When did you get all this?" Bree asked, eyes moving from the television to the big monitor to her desk setup in the corner with the ring light and the microphone on its boom arm.

"A few months ago. Most of it."

"How do you afford all this?"

Jasmine looked around the room at the inherited table, the thrifted chairs, the shelves she could disassemble in twenty minutes. Then she remembered fourteen trips down four flights of stairs carrying outdated electronics. And that one single thing that sparked it all. Bree's ring light still in the original box, being moved to yet another apartment, never once even turned on.

She looked at Bree with the slow sideways smile of someone who had been waiting a year for this exact conversation. Then Jasmine instructed, "Why don't you pull up a chair? I've got a lot to tell you."

What Jasmine Learned

The story Jasmine grew up with was simple: own things, keep things, and eventually success takes care of itself.

Adult life turned out to be less permanent than the people teaching those lessons expected.

For Jasmine, lease-to-own was never about being unable to buy. It was about keeping options open in a world where technology, careers, relationships, and priorities changed faster than they used to. After enough moving boxes, enough outdated electronics, and enough Saturdays spent sweating through stairwells, she learned something ownership had never really taught her.

Sometimes the smartest thing you can own is flexibility.

Current is still growing. The ring light is still on.

* * *

Chapter 17

Dirt Roads and Pride

Wade grew up in a house with four kids, one bathroom, and constant chatter.

Three younger sisters guaranteed that.

By the time he was twelve, he could braid hair badly, knew more about dance recitals than most boys his age, and had learned that if you wanted leftovers in a house that crowded, hesitation was expensive. His sisters called him overprotective. Wade called it realistic. He spent half his childhood driving them places, fixing broken things for them, and pretending he was annoyed when they borrowed his hoodies.

Truth was, he liked being needed.

His dad worked construction for nearly thirty years and believed strongly in two things: show up early and take care of your tools. Wade grew up hearing both ideas so often they stopped sounding like advice and started sounding like natural laws.

Some of his earliest memories happened from the passenger seat of old trucks.

He remembered cold mornings before school when his father stopped for gas station coffee and let Wade hold the paper cup because it made him feel older. He remembered handing wrenches to his dad while pretending he understood what the tools did. He remembered learning that men sometimes said very little when they loved each other.

Mostly, they worked beside each other.

In high school, Wade wasn't the loud guy or the star athlete. He played defensive end for two years because coaches liked boys who worked hard and didn't complain. He dated a little. Mostly, he worked. Summers were spent hauling materials, cleaning job sites, and saving money because his father believed teenagers with paychecks stayed out of trouble.

Weekends belonged to trucks.

At seventeen, Wade's uncle took him down a dirt trail forty minutes outside town and changed the course of his life without realizing it.

The first creek crossing hooked him.

The smell of wet dirt, hot brakes, pine trees, and river water mingled into something Wade still couldn't explain years later. Out there, phones stopped mattering. Bills stopped mattering. Nobody cared what clothes you wore or how much money you made. The trail cared whether you picked the right line and whether your truck could handle what came next.

Wade loved that immediately.

At twenty-six, he bought his own truck after saving for three years. It was exactly the kind of truck a young tradesman dreams about owning. Big enough for work. Strong enough for towing. Reliable enough that his father nodded approvingly when Wade pulled into the driveway.

That nod mattered more than Wade admitted.

Monday through Friday, the truck worked.

It hauled tools, lumber, compressors, and equipment to job sites all over town. It backed into muddy lots, pulled trailers, and sat in places most vehicles never saw. Wade depended on it the same way carpenters depend on saws or welders depend on torches. When your reputation is still being built, showing up matters.

Friday evenings were different.

Friday evenings belonged to trails.

For two years, though, Wade knew something was missing.

The factory tires handled pavement fine and job sites adequately, but trails exposed weaknesses quickly. He had gotten stuck twice. He had crossed creeks holding his breath more times than he cared to count. He had watched friends glide through mud sections while he worked around limitations he knew his truck shouldn't have.

The frustrating part was that Wade already knew exactly what he needed.

He wanted serious all terrain tires mounted on beadlock wheels. Something that could survive muddy job sites during the week and rocky trails on weekends without forcing him to compromise.

He also knew what those setups cost.

Wade was responsible with money, which often means fun things wait. Business money came first. Emergency savings came first. Truck maintenance came first. The upgrade fund moved slowly because adulthood tends to move slowly.

One Tuesday afternoon at a job site, while pulling nails from scrap boards and finishing cold coffee, another tradesman casually mentioned lease-to-own options for tires and wheels.

Wade stopped what he was doing.

"Say that again."

Research came first because research always came first.

Wade spent nights watching reviews, reading agreements, and comparing numbers because he had no interest in signing paperwork he didn't understand. What he found surprised him by making sense immediately. Weekly payments fit his budget. Damage protection mattered. Repair coverage mattered even more. The choice to acquire ownership whenever he wanted mattered most because Wade liked knowing his stuff was his.

Saturday morning he reviewed and signed the lease-purchase agreement. In almost no time, he was walking slowly around his truck in the parking lot wearing a big grin.

People who spend their weekends on the trail understand this feeling.

Sometimes new wheels and tires aren't just an upgrade. They're permission to stop wondering if the truck can make it—and start wondering where to go next.

He drove straight to the trails. The first creek crossing told him everything. For years, crossing that section required concentration and a little luck. Wade picked careful lines, feathered the throttle, and silently negotiated with equipment that was never fully up to the task.

This time the truck simply worked. The tires bit into the creek bed. The wheels held their line. The truck moved forward exactly where Wade pointed it. He reached the other side and stopped.

The engine idled softly. Water moved around rocks nearby.

For a moment, Wade just sat there.

Two years of compromise disappeared during thirty seconds of traction. He stayed out three extra hours.

Things changed at work too. Job sites felt easier. Mud stopped creating anxiety. Backing trailers onto uneven ground became less stressful. The truck looked more serious now too, and in the trades appearance matters more than outsiders realize. Proper equipment tells people you know what you are doing before you ever say a word.

Co-workers noticed. His father noticed too.

One Sunday afternoon, Wade was helping rotate his dad's tires in the driveway. His dad turned around and looked at Wade's truck behind farther down the driveway. He just nodded.

"Looks like you finally got it set up right."

That sentence stayed with Wade for weeks.

After eight months or so, a strong run of jobs left Wade some extra cash. The choice to acquire ownership of his wheels and tires was now a no-brainer. He made them his outright. Exactly like he wanted.

Friday evenings now find him driving thirty minutes toward dirt roads that eventually become no roads at all. His friends still pile into trucks afterward and stand around coolers talking about trails, suspension setups, and whose recovery strap saved the day.

His sisters still call when things break. His dad still asks how work is going. And creek crossings are not questions anymore.

They are just part of the drive.

What Wade Learned

Wade will tell you tires and wheels changed the truck.

That is true.

But what really changed was how often he had to work around limitations that no longer made sense.

Lease-purchase worked because Wade's life needed equipment before his savings timeline could catch up. It gave him the setup when the truck needed it, protected him when repairs mattered, and let ownership happen when the timing worked for him.

His truck still works for a living.

So does Wade.

One finally caught up with the other.

* * *

Chapter 18

Let's Make It Work for You

You've made it this far, and I hope something in these pages has started to feel like a breath of fresh air.

Now the natural question is: How do you actually use this in your own life? How do you decide when access makes sense for you, without feeling overwhelmed or like you're doing something wrong?

Let's talk about it the way you might talk with a good friend. Honestly, without pressure, and with your real life in mind.

Before You Give It a Try

Before you walk into any store or agree to a lease-to-own arrangement, pause and ask yourself this:

“Does owning this make my life better right now?”

Not ‘Can I afford it eventually?’

Not ‘Is this what everyone else does?’

Just that one simple question.

Sometimes the honest answer is yes, and that’s wonderful. Ownership can feel deeply satisfying when it truly fits your life.

The Unique Elegance and Design

Before moving forward, one practical clarity will serve you well throughout everything that follows and it is one that most consumer guides to lease-to-own never quite get around to stating plainly.

The lease-to-own model is specifically designed for durable goods: products that can be taken home, used, returned if necessary, and re-leased to another customer. That is not an arbitrary limit. It is the legal and logical foundation of what makes the entire model work. The reason there is no debt, no interest, no credit required, and no long-term obligation. Because the product can be returned, the transaction does not need to function like a loan. Because the product can be re-leased, the provider can absorb the risk that conventional financing cannot. The reason the whole thing works.

Everything that makes it flexible, accessible, and easy to walk away from, rests on this foundation.

Durable goods that fit the model include furniture, appliances, electronics, tires and wheels, HVAC systems, storage buildings, mobility devices, and the wide range of other products described throughout this book. What these products share is that they can be maintained, returned, refurbished, and redeployed, which is precisely what allows the model's service and maintenance commitment to function as it does.

Services alone fall outside the model's design. A service contract with no durable good attached is a different transaction, with different legal and financial characteristics. Where services appear in lease-to-own arrangements, they are incidental to the product: installation, maintenance, repair, and support tied directly to the item itself.

RNR's complete Customer Care Package, which at many locations includes: professional installation, lifetime rotations and balance, flat repair, nitrogen, alignment checks, and 12 months of roadside assistance, is a clear example. The tires are the durable good. The services support the tires. That relationship makes complete sense and gives you a little warm feeling inside knowing someone genuinely has your back. A true value to you.

When a standalone service subscription without a product at its center is offered, it's a different thing entirely and would fall outside the lease-to-own model as this book describes it.

One additional boundary is worth knowing about clearly. Pets have been explored in the past as a potential lease-to-own category and are specifically not something the industry supports. Pet leasing raises significant legal and ethical issues and is explicitly prohibited in several states, including California and potentially others.

This is an appropriate and clear line: lease-to-own was built for durable goods, not living creatures. Any arrangement purporting to offer lease-to-own terms on a pet is not operating within the legitimate, regulated model this book describes and is worth treating with the same skepticism you would apply to any offer that doesn't fit the *Four Core Truths*.

Knowing these boundaries does not limit your use of this model. It protects it for you, and for the millions of other consumers whose trust the best operators in this industry have spent decades earning.

The Power of the Early Exit

The option to acquire ownership early is a great tool for anyone who wants to minimize their total cost and own outright. This is covered in most all the State statutes that regulate the rental-purchase transaction. The action appears with various names across the State laws. The terminology shows up as: "ownership option," "buyout option," "early purchase option," and choosing to "acquire ownership."

If your provider is reputable and follows the statutes of their State, they will offer some form of early exit. This is the ability to exit your lease-purchase agreement ahead of the full term at a reduced total cost. The standard industry benchmark is 90 days, and for most consumers exercising this option within that window can bring their total cost very close to, or in some cases equal to, the retail cash price of the product.

However, most customer-focused providers go further. RNR Tire Express locations, for example, offer windows at 30, 60, 90 days, or even 4-months-same-as-cash. They tailor to each customer's financial timeline. In essence, a person with a tire or wheel lease from RNR can buy out their contract at any time during the process. In fact 90% of their customers do choose to take the early buy-out because of the money savings it offers. The customer is always in control and the choice is always their own.

Before you move forward, ask your service agent specifically about every early-purchase window available at that location and compare the total cost at each window to the retail price. Then assess honestly which window your cash flow can realistically support and choose accordingly.

If none of the standard options align with your timeline, ask whether a tailored plan is possible. The answer may surprise you. And if no window is currently within reach, understand the full-term cost clearly before committing. Whether you choose to take an early-purchase or buy-out should fit your life, not the other way around.

Your Reinstatement Right — Built-in Safety Net

There is one feature of the rent-to-own model that almost nobody talks about and that may be the single most important consumer protection in the entire arrangement. As mentioned earlier, according to the APRO website, 97% of rent-to-own stores provide lifetime reinstatement options or rights. This lifetime reinstatement feature allows customers to return a product and later re-rent the same item while receiving credit for payments already made. It is simply the chance to get your lease-purchase agreement back on track or push the restart button.

Here is what it means in plain language: if life throws you a curveball, like a job loss, a medical bill, a family emergency, any of the unexpected disruptions that arrive without warning in every life, and you are unable to keep up with your payments and have to return your item, you don't lose everything you have already paid.

Within a set window of time, which varies by state but typically ranges from 30 to 180 days, you can come back to your RTO store, catch up on the payments you missed plus any applicable fees, and resume your agreement right where you left off. Your payment history is preserved. Your progress toward ownership is preserved. The door stays open.

Life happens. We know that. Come back when you can. We'll be here waiting.

Jerome — The Bookmark

Jerome had been counting down the weeks like chapters in a favorite book. For those first four months he had walked into the store every payday, handing over his lease payment for the dryer that had single-handedly transformed his family's routine. He knew he could pay by using his phone, but there was something about stopping by that completed his week.

Before the dryer had arrived, laundry day meant loading wet clothes into baskets, driving to the laundromat with the kids in tow, waiting for machines, and hauling everything back home. His apartment complex didn't allow clothes lines, so the laundromat trips had become a weekly ordeal. Folding clothes on sticky tables while trying to keep the children entertained. The new dryer changed all that. Now he could wash at home and dry in one smooth process. Warm towels, soft sheets, and the simple pleasure of finishing laundry without driving somewhere had become part of the rhythm of their home.

Then life turned the page unexpectedly. His hours were cut, and the numbers no longer added up. With a heavy heart, he called the store, explained the situation with tired but honest words, and returned the dryer. It wasn't just an appliance he was giving back. It felt like handing over a piece of his hard-won and finally-found stability.

Three months later, the storm had passed. His paycheck had grown steady again. He walked back through those familiar doors, half-afraid of what he'd find. He happily found that his past lease payments were not lost. Those months of payments had been carefully preserved like a bookmark left exactly where he had stopped reading. The lease-purchase agreement was waiting for him, patient and unchanged.

He picked up where he had left off. That first load of laundry after reinstatement felt almost ceremonial. As the dryer hummed and the warm, fresh scent of tumbled clothes even spilled out into the into the living room, Jerome couldn't hold back his huge grin and sigh of relief. The dryer was back. The routine was back. And once again, his family had both precious hours of their week restored and that small but meaningful piece of normalcy returned.

That is the quiet power of this model. It doesn't demand perfection. It offers understanding and a second chance when life needs one.

Linda — The Fun That Came Back

For Linda, a single mother in Tennessee, home was the sound of her children laughing after a long school day. Every afternoon they would burst through the door, kick off their shoes, and head straight for the living room. The gaming console had quickly become the heart of their evenings. Controllers in hand, shouts of excitement, and high-fives whenever someone completed a level. It was their special time together, the one part of the day when the worries of the world faded and it was just the three of them, playing, teasing, and bonding.

Then came the sudden round of layoffs at her company. When the notice arrived, Linda knew she could no longer keep up with the weekly payments. With a heavy heart, she called the store, explained the situation, and returned the gaming console in the same careful condition she had always kept it.

It felt like more than a game system leaving. The living room suddenly felt silent and emptier. The kids still whined about it, but she usually just tried to change the subject, her chest tight with guilt.

A short time later, when her new job had stabilized, Linda walked back into the store, half-afraid of what she would find. But the payments she had previously made were still there, securely recorded. The rental-purchase agreement picked up exactly where it had left off.

She brought it back home that afternoon.

That first evening, as her children rushed in from the bus, their eyes lit up when they saw the familiar black box hooked up to the TV. Controllers in hand, laughter filled the room again. They played, shouted, giggled, and for the first time in weeks their home felt alive. Homework could wait just a little longer tonight. This was their time.

That wasn't just a game system returning. That was joy returning to their evenings. That was the sound of her kids being kids again. And for Linda, that was everything.

Mark — Oh What a Relief It Is

Mark had always taken pride in his yard. After long shifts at the factory, he liked coming home to a neat, well-kept lawn. It was something he could control when the rest of life felt unpredictable. But at fifty-two, his knees were no longer as dependable as they once were. The old push mower had become a punishing ritual. Every weekend he would finish the yard exhausted, his knees throbbing as the cartilage took a beating from hours of walking and twisting. The next day he would move slowly, barely able to climb stairs or even bend to tie his shoes without wincing.

He needed something better. A zero-turn riding mower would cut his mowing time in half and finally give his aging knees some relief from another brutal Georgia summer. But with tight bills and no extra cash for a big purchase, the price tag felt completely out of reach.

Rent-to-own gave him a way forward. He walked into the store, explained what he was looking for, and left the same day with a powerful zero-turn mower on weekly payments that fit his paycheck.

The first time he fired it up, the difference was immediate. The mower glided smoothly across the grass, turning on a dime around trees and flower beds. He finished the entire yard in under an hour instead of three. For the first time in years, he climbed off the mower without aching knees. A nice trimmed lawn no longer left him incapacitated for the rest of the weekend.

Then summer ended. The grass stopped growing, the leaves fell, and money got even tighter. Mark knew he wouldn't need the mower again until spring. With a touch of regret, he called the store and returned it for the winter months.

When his beloved grass started perking up again in the early spring, Mark returned to the store. The payments he had already made were still on record. They reinstated the rental-purchase agreement right where he had left off.

That first warm Saturday, when the zero-turn mower was delivered again, Mark felt a wave of relief. He was so eager to climbed on, start up the engine, and smile as it hummed beneath him. His knees were now free to remain steady and strong as he made the effortless passes across the yard. The lawn looked better than ever when he completed that first mow of the season.

As he put the mower away that evening, he realized this tool wasn't just making his weekends easier, it was protecting his body and giving him back a little control and dignity, season after season, exactly when he needed it. Without the rent-to-own option, he would never have known this kind of relief.

> NOTE: To understand the specific reinstatement window that applies in your state, see the State-By-State Consumer Guide to RTO Protections at the back of this book.

Aligning Payments with Your Paycheck Cycle

Most RTO providers will work with you to align your payment due date with your actual paycheck cycle. This is not a minor convenience. Having a payment come due three days before payday rather than three days after it can mean the difference between a smooth, stress-free experience and a missed payment that can cause a headache you didn't need.

When establishing your rental-purchase agreement, raise this proactively. Ask your service agent about aligning your payment due date with your paycheck schedule. A good service agent will often raise it themselves before you move agree to their paperwork. If they don't, raise it yourself.

The Digital Closet

Professional organizers have a simple rule for tackling an overflowing closet: if you haven't worn it in the last year, it goes. Resell it, donate it, or let it go. The question isn't whether you liked it once. The question is whether it's serving you now.

Your subscriptions deserve the same honest look.

The access economy makes it beautifully easy to sign up for things, like a streaming service here, a software tool there, a meal kit you tried for a month and then forgot about. Each one is a small number that can add up dependably, month after month, on autopilot.

The living lighter principle applies here just as much as it applies to your furniture or your storage building. Go through your subscriptions the way a good organizer goes through your closet. Ask one simple question about each one: have I actually used this in the last month? If the answer is no, then cancel it. No guilt. No hesitation. That's not a failure of commitment. That's exactly what the access model is designed to allow.

The target was never to subscribe to everything. The real objective was to access what genuinely serves your life right now, and to let go of what doesn't, cleanly and without looking back.

Weekly, Bi-Weekly, or Monthly Payments?

Most providers offer many payment pacing options. Match your payment to be timed with your income frequency, whether weekly, bi-weekly, or monthly. Confirm your payment amount and your due date, and if that date doesn't align naturally with your paycheck cycle, ask for an adjustment before you move forward. Most will say yes before you finish asking.

The aim is to make your RTO payment feel like a natural, frictionless part of your financial rhythm rather than a disruption to it.

Ready to Try Lease-Purchase?

Before embracing any lease-purchase or rental-purchase agreement, it helps to return to the *Four Core Truths* introduced in Chapter 1, because they are not just principles for the industry to live by, they are an easy way for you to decide on any agreement you are considering.

Is this arrangement free of debt and long-term obligation? Is it genuinely flexible and choice-based? Does it provide essential access with dignity, without requiring traditional credit? And is the provider regulated and transparent under your state's specific RTO statute?

If the answer to all four is yes, you are likely evaluating a legitimate, regulated arrangement built to protect you. For the full legal and historical story of how this regulatory support structure came to be, including the honest account of what skeptics got right and what changed, see the back of this book. That said, not every provider is equal. Some operate without APRO affiliation, without proper training, or without the professional standards the best operators have built their reputations on.

The APRO *Four Core Truths* of the RTO industry are your filter. Use them.

The APRO website distills them to four phrases to remember:

1. No Debt / No Obligation
2. Flexible and Choice-Based
3. Essential Access and Dignity
4. Regulated and Transparent

If the store you are considering lives by all four, you are in the right place. If something feels off or doesn't seem to fit any one of them, ask more questions or shop elsewhere.

Before you commit, ask the service agent to show you, in writing, the options you have to acquire ownership. Ask how the reinstatement right works in practice at that specific location. Ask what happens if you miss a payment and what the exact fees are. Ask whether the store offers any maintenance or repair service as part of the agreement and how that service works if you were to need it.

Here's something worth saying plainly: lease-to-own isn't limited to life's necessities. It also works beautifully for life's upgrades.

Not everything that improves your life is essential. Sometimes it's a more comfortable sofa, a larger television, a better camera, or a set of wheels you've dreamed about for years. These aren't the things that keep life functioning. They're the things that make it richer, more comfortable, or simply more fun.

Life isn't built only on necessities. It's also shaped by the experiences and comforts that make ordinary days a little better.

And if you decide it's not for you, your credit isn't affected. If it delights you, choose to own it. If it doesn't, return it and move on. That is not impulsive. That is intelligent. RTO may be the only place in a buyer's life where you are genuinely free to say yes to a want without consequence.

The model works best when you treat it as a tool rather than a permanent solution. Use it when you need immediate access and flexibility. Return the item when your circumstances change. Reinstate when you are ready again. The door is designed to stay open.

Once you feel you have a handle on the benefits and options, you are cleared for takeoff. You aren't just ready to enter the RTO experience, you are ready to use one of the most flexible, accessible, and genuinely people-friendly tools available today.

Confidently. Intentionally. On your own terms.

That is not just smart shopping.

That is thriving.

* * *

Chapter 19

Living Lighter

You've done the reading. You've met the families. You've seen the math. And somewhere in these pages, hopefully, something has shifted, even just a little, in the way you think about what it means to live well.

The finish line was never the deed in the drawer or the receipt in the filing cabinet. It was always something simpler and more personal than that. It was the life happening inside the walls. Warm, flexible, and entirely your own.

What This Means for You

The future belongs to those who understand they have choices.

You don't have to follow the old script that says you must own everything to be successful. You can build a comfortable, functional, even beautiful home while keeping more choices alive and less heaviness on your shoulders.

You can enjoy the sofa your family snuggles on, a refrigerator that keeps your casseroles chilled, safe tires that grip on rain-slick roads, without tying up all your resources or carrying the worry and responsibilities that come with full ownership.

Access gives you permission to live in the present while staying ready for whatever comes next. It lets you enjoy what improves your days right now, without forcing you to commit to a version of life that might not fit six months or six years from now.

Be Your Own Hero — Go Live It

At the end of the day, this isn't really about mattresses, dishwashers or tires.

It's about how you want to live.

Do you want more breathing room? More freedom to adjust when life changes? More time and energy for your loved-ones and the moments that truly matter?

Now you know. Access is waiting for you, and so is the chance to become the hero of your own story.

It's not the only way. Ownership still makes perfect sense for many things and for many people. The point isn't to reject ownership completely. Tt's to recognize that it's no longer the only smart choice.

You now have options. You can mix and match what works best for your family, your budget, your season of life.

That freedom is powerful.

So, as you close this book, I hope you carry these simple ideas with you:

You deserve a home that feels good to live in.

You deserve modern daily conveniences and tools that respect your real circumstances.

You deserve the freedom to upgrade your life, not just your stuff, whenever something more aligned with the way you want to live comes along.

And access is simply one more way to make that possible.

Live lighter.

Live intentionally.

And build the warm, full life you truly want. Infinitely. On your own terms.

* * *

How Skeptics Forged a Superior RTO

If You've Heard Differing Claims

If you have spent any time searching online for information about rent-to-own, you have probably seen some version of this story: that the industry takes advantage of people, charges high rates, and uses the law to punish customers who fall behind.

Those stories deserve attention. A reader who asks hard questions is a reader who protects herself.

This section gives the rest of the picture. It appears near the back of the book because the heart of *Infinite Upgrades* is the stories of real families. But honest answers belong here too.

The Wrong Pair of Glasses

Most of the people who criticized rent-to-own over the years were consumer advocates who believed they were protecting families.

They saw rent-to-own and assumed it was a loan in disguise. That assumption led them to attempt to calculate an effective annual interest rate by comparing total payments to the cash price. The resulting number often looked alarming.

As this book has said repeatedly, rent-to-own is not a loan. It is a lease.

The same basic arrangement used when renting an apartment or a car, or when earlier generations rented their telephone from AT&T for decades.

What the Law Actually Said

This wasn't just a philosophical argument. It played out in courtrooms and statehouses across America for decades. And the results were consistent.

By the time the dust had largely settled, 47 states had passed laws specifically recognizing rent-to-own as a lease. Not a loan, not a credit sale. Federal legislation defined rental-purchase agreements as something separate from the credit transactions covered by the Truth in Lending Act. The Consumer Leasing Act, which is the federal law that covers leases, doesn't even apply to RTO, because its short-term, week-to-week or month-to-month structure puts it outside the law's scope entirely.

Consumer advocacy groups pushed back hard. Some state courts agreed with them. New Jersey, Minnesota, and Wisconsin treated RTO more like a credit sale, and those states' laws reflect that. The industry acknowledges this openly. In those states, RTO operates under consumer credit rules rather than rental-purchase laws. The protection is different, but it's still there

Everywhere else, the argument was examined carefully and the lease held up, because a lease is what it is.

APRO, the national trade association for the RTO industry, founded in 1980, spent decades making this case in legislatures and courts. Not because they were powerful. Because they were right.

Where the Skeptics Had a Point

Honest people do not pretend every criticism was wrong. Some of it was not.

In the early years, some agreements were harder to understand than they should have been. Not all customers fully understood the total cost of completing an rent-to-own agreement or what would happen if they missed a payment.

Some operators used the threat of legal action as a collection tool. That is not what the model is supposed to be.

The best operators never operated that way. They still don't.

Knowing the difference between a store that has your back and one that does not is part of why this book exists.

Compared to What?

Back to those attempted effective interest rate calculations. The skeptics who tried to run those numbers were not lying. The math was real. But it was like trying to find the effective interest rate for the apartment rent you are paying every month. What was missing in their attempts was context.

The calculation only matters if the customer had a lower-cost alternative available. For most rent-to-own customers, the real choice was between rent-to-own and doing without the item entirely.

And if the comparison is a high-interest store credit card (the actual alternative for many customers who have one), the picture changes. Store cards at major retailers charge 29.99 to 34.99 percent interest, lock you in, make you responsible for every repair, and offer no easy way to walk away.

From this standpoint, the criticism could seem a bit more like a blind spot than analysis.

Social Media and the Stories That Spread

The legal debate, whatever you think of it, was conducted by people who had fully read the agreements and had formed various arguments to be worked out. What has happened in the era of social media is something very different.

A quick search for "rent-to-own scam" returns posts that apply interest rate math without any context, blame the entire industry for the behavior of its worst actors, cite stories from decades ago as if nothing has changed, and ignore ownership choice options, reinstatement rights, and the simple fact that most customers don't complete every payment. The majority use the model as a short-term tool and exit early.

None of those posts compare RTO to the cable modem sitting on the customer's router shelf. The one she's been renting for $15 a month for five years, for a device she could own for $100, with no buyout ever offered and nobody saying a word about it.

The person most hurt by a careless social media post isn't the industry. It's the mother who reads it at midnight, feels ashamed of the one tool that was an option available to her, and drives to work the next morning on tires she knows aren't safe.

Misinformation has a cost. It's paid by the people who needed the truth.

Where Things Stand Today

The industry operating today is not the industry those early critics were describing.

Forty-seven states now have specific laws governing rent-to-own transactions. Reinstatement rights, early purchase options, and required disclosures of total costs are standard in most states. The best protection any customer has is understanding how the transaction works, knowing your rights, and asking the right questions before you move forward.

Today, 47 states have specific laws governing RTO transactions. APRO's 50-state Model Lease Agreement Library, which was developed with the compliance law firm Hudson Cook, LLP and launched in 2026, gives member operators clear, legally current agreements built around transparency and customer rights. Reinstatement rights protect customers who miss payments. As were have stated before, early buy-out/purchase options exist in every reputable store. Disclosure of total costs is required by law in most states.

Dr. Charles Smitherman has spent much of his career documenting the rent-to-own evolution. He is an attorney who holds a law degree (JD) from the University of Georgia and Doctor of Philosophy (PhD) in International Law and Legal Studies from the University of Oxford. He is also credentialed as a Certified Association Executive (CAE), Certified Franchise Executive (CFE), and privacy professional (CIPP/US, CIPM).

For the definitive legal and historical account of the industry's development, I highly recommend that you read Dr. Charles Smitherman's book *The Rent-to-Own Revolution: A Definitive History of Advocacy and Consumer Access*. It's the most complete account available, detailing how the industry responded to its critics, won its key legal battles, and helped build the strong consumer protections we have today. If you want the deeper legal backstory, this is the book to read.

And Most Importantly

The best protection any RTO customer has is exactly what this book has tried to give you: an understanding of how the transaction works, a clear sense of your rights, and the confidence to ask the right questions before you move forward.

A good store welcomes those questions. It aligns your payments with your paycheck. It explains the reinstatement policy before you need it. It shows up when something breaks. It knows your name.

The skeptics were measuring the wrong thing. They counted what flexibility costs and never got around to counting what it's worth.

The mother who walked in needing cold milk for her children, and walked out with her dignity intact and a refrigerator humming in her kitchen, knew the difference.

For your specific consumer rights in your state, see the section State-By-State Consumer Guide to RTO Protections that follows.

* * *

Your Guide to RTO Protections

Your Rights as a Consumer — In Every State

Rent-to-own, also known as lease-to-own, RTO and LTO, is one of the most regulated consumer arrangements in American retail. Unlike credit cards, installment loans, or store financing, rent-to-own is structured as a lease.

Bottom line: In almost every state you can return the item anytime, get your item fixed for free while you have it, and you're never stuck with debt

Four foundational consumer protections apply across virtually every jurisdiction in the United States:

No Debt, No Obligation. Rent-to-own is a lease, not a loan. There is no credit needed, no loan, no interest, and no long-term financial commitment. You are never locked in beyond your next payment.

Flexible and Choice-Based. You may return the item at any time. Most states provide reinstatement rights, meaning that if you miss a payment or need to return an item temporarily, you can reclaim it later by catching up on what you owe, without losing credit for payments already made.

Essential Access and Dignity. While you have possession of the item, the RTO provider is typically responsible for service, maintenance, and repairs at no additional cost to you, protecting you from unexpected repair bills and keeping the arrangement truly worry-free.

Regulated and Transparent. 47 states have enacted specific rental-purchase and lease-purchase statutes requiring clear written disclosures of all costs, payment terms, and consumer rights before moving forward. The remaining three states: Minnesota, New Jersey, and Wisconsin, classify these agreements as credit sales, subjecting them to their consumer credit and lending laws, which in many cases provide equally strong or stronger protections. The Federal Trade Commission provides additional federal oversight across all states.

One detail worth knowing as you read your own state's entry: while every state regulates this transaction, they don't all call it by the same name.

Depending on where you live, the contract you sign may be called a **Rental-Purchase Agreement**, a **Lease-Purchase Agreement**, or a **Rent-to-Own Agreement** — three different legal labels for the same basic consumer protection. Whichever term your state uses, the substance is the same: you're never required to keep paying, you can walk away at any time by returning the item, and you have a clear, legally defined path to acquiring ownership if and when you choose to.

What follows is a state-by-state summary of how these protections work where you live. Whether you are considering your first rent-to-own arrangement or simply want to understand your rights, this reference is designed to give you the confidence to make informed decisions. If you ever have questions about the terms of a specific agreement, your state's consumer protection office is an excellent resource and a reputable RTO provider will always welcome your questions before you move forward.

And a very important fact needs to be made clear before you read the information provided for your own state. Please remember that laws change and the material presented in the book is only educational and is not to be taken as legal advice.

Alabama

(Ala. Code §§8-25-1 to 8-25-6)

Alabama's law governs what it calls a **Rental-Purchase Agreement** under the Rental-Purchase Agreements Act. It requires clear written disclosures of the cash price, the total payments needed to acquire ownership, and all other key terms. You receive immediate possession while making affordable payments, with the merchant retaining title until you complete all payments or otherwise comply with the ownership terms of the agreement. You may end the arrangement at any time by returning the merchandise. If you miss a payment, reinstatement rights allow you to catch up — typically within 5 days for monthly agreements or 2 days for more frequent schedules — by paying past-due amounts plus any allowed late fee. If a merchant violates the law, you may recover actual damages plus 25% of total payments to acquire ownership, plus attorney fees and court costs. Alabama's framework gives consumers strong transparency and a meaningful second chance, making RTO a safe and practical path to ownership without long-term debt.

Alaska

(Alaska Stat. §§45.35.010 to 45.35.099)

Alaska calls this transaction a **Lease-Purchase Agreement**, governed under the state's "Lease-Purchases of Personal Property" chapter. The law requires clear disclosures and aligns fully with consumer protection standards. You gain immediate possession while the lessor holds title until all payments necessary to acquire ownership are complete. The agreement is fully terminable at any time simply by returning the item — there is no obligation beyond your next payment. Reinstatement rights are notably generous — 21 days if fewer than two-thirds of payments have been made, and 45 days if more — giving Alaskans real flexibility to reclaim their item after a temporary setback. This structure keeps every option open and ensures that a missed payment never means a permanent loss.

Arizona

(Ariz. Rev. Stat. §§44-6801 to 44-6814)

Arizona regulates the **Rental-Purchase Agreement** and mandates prominent point-of-sale tags disclosing the cash price, periodic payment amount, and total payments required to acquire ownership. You may return the item at any time, ending the agreement with no further obligation, and reinstatement is available within 7 days by paying past-due amounts plus reasonable pickup/redelivery and a reinstatement fee. If a merchant fails to follow the rules, remedies include the greater of actual damages or 25% of total payments (between $100 and $1,000), plus attorney fees. Arizona consumers can approach RTO with confidence that the terms are transparent and that a path back is always available if life gets in the way.

Arkansas

(Ark. Code Ann. §§4-92-101 to 4-92-107)

Arkansas's **Rental-Purchase Agreement** statute requires clear contract disclosures and provides reinstatement rights within 5 business days for monthly agreements, or 2 business days for more frequent schedules, by paying past-due amounts or returning the item. Title remains with the merchant until you acquire ownership through full payment or by complying with the agreement's ownership terms. Remedies for violations include actual damages plus 25% of total payments (between $100 and $1,000), plus attorney fees and costs. Arkansas families can use RTO confidently for immediate possession, knowing that a temporary financial setback does not mean a permanent loss.

California

(Cal. Civ. Code §§1812.620 to 1812.650 — Karnette Rental-Purchase Act)

California provides some of the most robust consumer protections in the country for what its law calls a **Rental-Purchase Agreement**. Point-of-sale tags must display cash price, payments, and total cost to acquire ownership in a clear boxed format. Total payments are capped at 2.25 times the cash price in many cases, providing a built-in ceiling on what you can be asked to pay. You receive possession immediately and may return the item at any time. California also gives you the statutory right to acquire ownership early — within three months of signing — by paying the cash price minus the payments you've already made. Reinstatement rights are generous, typically extending to the end of the 10th day after a due date or longer in some cases. Violations allow recovery of actual damages, 25% of payments to acquire ownership (between $100 and $1,000), attorney fees, costs, and potential additional damages for willful acts. California's price limits, early-ownership right, and strong reinstatement protections make RTO a transparent, capped-cost option for families who need access without overcommitment.

Colorado

(Colo. Rev. Stat. §§5-10-101 to 5-10-1001 — Colorado Rental Purchase Agreement Act)

Colorado's law governs the **Rental Purchase Agreement** and emphasizes clear contracts and meaningful reinstatement rights. The statute even devotes an entire section — titled, simply, "Acquiring Ownership" — to spelling out exactly when and how a lessee may acquire ownership of the property, including through an early buy-out option that can reduce your total cost. If you surrender an item and later wish to reclaim it, reinstatement is available within 60 days — or up to 120 days if more than 60% of payments have been made. You gain possession and use while the agreement is active, with ownership available only after completing payments or exercising the buy-out option. Remedies include actual damages plus the greater of $250 or 25% of total cost to acquire ownership, plus attorney fees. These safeguards help Coloradans access essentials flexibly while preserving every future option.

Connecticut

(Conn. Gen. Stat. §§42-240 to 42-253)

Connecticut is one of a handful of states that does not use the term "rental-purchase agreement" at all

— its statute is titled, and governs, the **Rent-to-Own Agreement**. The law caps total payments at twice the cash price in many instances and requires point-of-sale tags with key cost information. Ownership transfers only upon completion of required payments — denominated in Connecticut law as the "rent-to-own price" — or through the lessee's statutory early purchase option. Notably, ownership automatically vests the moment 50% of all rental payments made equal the cash price of the property, at which point the agreement terminates. Reinstatement windows are exceptionally flexible: 30, 90, or 180 days depending on how many payments have been made. Remedies include actual damages (minimum $250), attorney fees, and costs. The price cap, automatic-ownership trigger, and extended reinstatement periods give Connecticut consumers exceptional reassurance that RTO remains affordable and recoverable.

Delaware

(Del. Code tit. 6, §§7601 to 7616 — Delaware Lease-Purchase Agreement Act)

Delaware calls this arrangement a **Lease-Purchase Agreement** and requires tags showing the cash price and total lease payments needed to acquire ownership. Reinstatement is available within 60 days if less than 60% of payments have been made, or within 180 days if more. Delaware's law gives you a statutory early purchase option: at any time after your first payment, you may acquire ownership by tendering 55% of the difference between the total payments necessary to acquire ownership and what you've already paid. Remedies for violations include the greater of actual damages or $300 (or 25% of payments), plus fees and costs, with a 10-day cure period for some violations. Delaware's balanced framework supports confident use of RTO with clear paths to possession and ownership alike.

Florida

(Fla. Stat. §§559.9231 to 559.9241)

Florida's **Rental-Purchase Agreement** law provides reinstatement within 60 days after the last timely payment if the item is surrendered promptly. Clear disclosures inform you of all costs to acquire ownership. Remedies include the greater of actual damages or 25% of total cost to acquire ownership, plus attorney fees and costs. Florida's second-chance provisions and consumer protections make RTO a practical, low-pressure way to gain possession of household essentials.

Georgia

(Ga. Code Ann. §§10-1-680 to 10-1-689)

Georgia is another state that does not use "rental-purchase agreement" terminology — its statute, Article 23 of the consumer protection code, defines and regulates the **Lease-Purchase Agreement**. Georgia provides reinstatement rights when no more than three payments have been missed and the item has been surrendered when requested. You receive possession immediately, with title remaining with the lessor until you exercise your option to purchase and become the owner of the property. Remedies are the greater of actual damages or $300 (or 25% of cost to acquire ownership), plus fees and costs. This practical framework gives Georgia families meaningful security during periods of cash-flow challenges.

Hawaii

(Haw. Rev. Stat. §§481M-1 to 481M-18)

Hawaii's chapter, "Lease-Purchase Agreements for Personal Property," governs the **Lease-Purchase Agreement**. It caps total payments at twice the cash price and provides reinstatement within 30 days after return, or 60 days if more than 60% of payments have been made. Clear disclosures and remedies — actual damages plus the greater of

$250 or 25% of total cost to acquire ownership — protect consumers. The price cap and extended reinstatement make Hawaii's framework especially consumer-friendly for gaining possession of household essentials without excessive cost.

Idaho

(Idaho Code §§28-36-101 to 28-36-111 — Idaho Lease-Purchase Agreement Act)

Idaho's law governs the **Lease-Purchase Agreement** and requires reinstatement within short windows — 5 days for monthly agreements or 2 days for more frequent schedules — by paying past-due amounts. Remedies allow actual damages or up to $1,000 for bad-faith violations. These straightforward rules help Idaho families confidently access items through RTO, knowing that lease terms — and the path to acquiring ownership — are fair and enforceable.

Illinois

(815 Ill. Comp. Stat. §§655/0.01 to 655/5 — Rental-Purchase Agreement Act)

Illinois mandates tags disclosing all amounts needed to acquire ownership of the item under its **Rental-Purchase Agreement** statute, and provides reinstatement before the later of one week or half the payment period. The law prohibits unfair terms including excessive late fees. Remedies include actual damages plus 25% of total payments ($250 to $1,000), plus attorney fees and costs. Illinois consumers benefit from strong disclosure requirements and reinstatement rights that keep control firmly in their hands.

Indiana

(Ind. Code §§24-7-1-1 to 24-7-9-7 — Indiana Rental Purchase Agreement Act)

Indiana's **Rental Purchase Agreement** law provides reinstatement rights if the item is surrendered and no more than 60 days have passed since its return. Remedies are the greater of actual damages, $300, or 25% of total payments necessary to acquire ownership, plus attorney fees. Hoosiers can use RTO with confidence, knowing they have a clear path to regain possession and meaningful legal recourse if anything goes wrong.

Iowa

(Iowa Code §§537.3601 to 537.3624)

Iowa's statute, found within its Consumer Credit Code, defines and governs the **Consumer Rental Purchase Agreement**. It requires disclosures identifying the transaction as a lease and detailing all payments needed to acquire ownership. Ownership is reached automatically — in a section of the law literally titled "Acquiring Ownership" — when 50% of all lease payments made equal the cash price under the statutory formula. Reinstatement is available within 60 days of return if the item has been surrendered. Remedies include the greater of actual damages or $300 (or 25% of total cost), plus fees. These rules ensure transparency and equity for Iowa consumers.

Kansas

(Kan. Stat. §§50-680 to 50-690)

Kansas, like Georgia and several other states, does not use "rental-purchase" terminology — its statute governs the **Lease-Purchase Agreement** and integrates RTO protections with the state's Consumer Protection Act, treating violations as unconscionable acts. Reinstatement is available within 5 days for monthly agreements or 2 days for more frequent schedules, by paying past-due amounts plus limited costs. Clear terms and accessible reinstatement — along with a defined path to becoming the owner of the property — give Kansas consumers dependable access through RTO, backed by the full weight of the state's consumer protection framework.

Kentucky

(Ky. Rev. Stat. §§367.976 to 367.985)

Kentucky's **Rental-Purchase Agreement** law provides reinstatement within 5 days for monthly agreements or 2 days for more frequent schedules, plus reasonable costs and a late fee. Remedies include actual damages plus 25% of total payments necessary to acquire ownership ($100 to $1,000), plus costs and attorney fees. Kentucky families can approach RTO with confidence in its fair and reasonable terms, and in a clear, statutorily defined path to ownership.

Louisiana

(La. Rev. Stat. §§9:3351 to 9:3362)

Louisiana's **Rental-Purchase Agreement** statute connects RTO protections to the state's Unfair Trade Practices Act, providing an additional layer of consumer recourse. Reinstatement is available within short grace periods — 5 days for monthly agreements or 2 days for more frequent schedules. Clear contracts, a defined path to acquiring ownership, and meaningful remedies under broader consumer protection law help Louisiana families use RTO safely for immediate possession of household essentials.

Maine

(Me. Rev. Stat. tit. 9-A, §§11-101 to 11-122)

Maine's law, Article 11 of its consumer credit code ("Rental-Purchase Practices"), governs the **Rental-Purchase Agreement**. It caps total payments at twice the cash price and requires placards disclosing key cost information, including whether an item is new or used. Maine law uses a precise defined term for the total buy-out cost — the "Total of payments to acquire ownership" — and ownership transfers only after payments reach that required threshold. Reinstatement is available within 7 days after a missed payment or upon request. Remedies include actual damages or $250 (whichever is greater), plus costs and attorney fees. Maine's price cap, defined buy-out term, and clear disclosures make RTO a reassuring and value-conscious option for Maine families.

Maryland

(Md. Code, Com. Law §§12-1101 to 12-1112 — Maryland Rental-Purchase Agreement Act)

Maryland requires tags showing renewal payments, total payments necessary to acquire ownership, and new/used status for what its law calls a **Rental-Purchase Agreement**. Maryland also gives consumers a statutory early purchase option to acquire ownership before completing all scheduled payments. Reinstatement is available within 5 days for monthly agreements or 2 days for weekly schedules, by paying past-due amounts plus a small fee (maximum $5). Remedies include actual damages plus $500, attorney fees, and costs. Maryland consumers enjoy straightforward, practical protections that make RTO a dependable choice.

Massachusetts

(Mass. Gen. Laws ch. 93, §§90 to 93)

Massachusetts is the one state where the operative statute doesn't define a "rental-purchase" or "lease-purchase" agreement at all — it defines and regulates the **Consumer Lease**, and the phrase "lease or rental-purchase agreement" appears only in passing, in the section covering advertising disclosures. Whatever it's called on paper, the substance is familiar: the law focuses on fair dealing, with reinstatement rights and remedies of actual damages plus 25% of total payments necessary to acquire ownership ($100 to $1,000), plus costs and attorney fees. The Bay State's consumer-oriented rules support flexible possession of household essentials without hidden risks or unexpected obligations.

Michigan

(Mich. Comp. Laws §§445.951 to 445.971)

As one of the earliest states to enact dedicated RTO legislation, Michigan's **Rental-Purchase Agreement Act** requires clear disclosures of the cash price and total payments needed to acquire ownership. You receive possession immediately and may terminate the agreement at any point without penalty. Ownership automatically vests once 45% of total periodic payments equal the disclosed cash price. Reinstatement rights allow you to revive your agreement by paying past-due amounts plus reasonable costs within statutory windows. Remedies include actual damages and attorney fees. Michigan's longstanding framework provides strong transparency and a reliable path forward for consumers.

Minnesota

Minnesota's statute does use the term "rental-purchase agreement," but Minnesota's courts have additionally classified these agreements as **credit sales** under the state's general consumer credit and retail installment sales laws (*Miller v. Colortyme*, 1994), layering an extra set of protections on top of the rental-purchase disclosures. This dual classification requires enhanced disclosures —

including effective cost information — and provides stronger remedies under lending statutes. Minnesota consumers benefit from these additional safeguards, which in many respects provide equal or greater protection than a standalone RTO statute, while the underlying agreement still uses "acquire ownership" language for the buy-out itself.

Mississippi

(Miss. Code Ann. §§75-24-151 to 75-24-175)

Mississippi's Rental-Purchase Agreement Act mandates clear disclosures of all terms and total payments needed to acquire ownership of property under a **Rental-Purchase Agreement**. Reinstatement is available within short grace periods by curing defaults. Remedies allow actual damages plus statutory penalties, attorney fees, and costs. These provisions support Mississippi families with transparency, flexibility, and meaningful recourse.

Missouri

(Mo. Rev. Stat. §§407.660 to 407.670)

Missouri's law — cited by name as the **"Rental-Purchase Agreement Act"** — requires point-of-sale and contract disclosures comparing the cash price to the total cost of acquiring ownership of the merchandise. Reinstatement rights and limits on repossession protect consumers from abrupt loss of possession. Remedies connect to the Merchandising Practices Act for damages and attorney fees. Missouri's framework provides practical safeguards for responsible and confident use of RTO.

Montana

(Mont. Code Ann. §§30-19-101 to 30-19-115 — Montana Rental-Purchase Agreement Act)

Montana's **Rental-Purchase Agreement** law emphasizes upfront disclosures and reinstatement options backed by scaled damages for violations. Any advertisement that mentions the right to acquire ownership of a specific item must clearly state that the transaction is a rental-purchase agreement and disclose the total payments required. The statute's focus on fair dealing gives Montana consumers a confident path to immediate possession of essential household goods while preserving full flexibility.

Nebraska

(Neb. Rev. Stat. §§69-2101 to 69-2119 — Consumer Rental Purchase Agreement Act)

Nebraska's law governs the **Consumer Rental Purchase Agreement** and mandates detailed disclosures and reinstatement rights by paying overdue amounts plus limited fees. Remedies include actual damages and attorney fees. These rules ensure that Nebraska consumers have the information and flexibility — and a clearly disclosed total cost to acquire ownership — that RTO is designed to deliver.

Nevada

(Nev. Rev. Stat. §§597.010 to 597.080)

Nevada is unique among the states: its statute doesn't use "rental-purchase agreement," "lease-purchase agreement," or "rent-to-own agreement" at all. It governs a **Lease Agreement with an Option to Purchase**, and even the consumer is given a different legal title here — Nevada law calls them a **"customer,"** not a "consumer." The law requires clear advertising and contract disclosures of total costs to acquire ownership of the leased property. Reinstatement provisions and prohibitions on unfair practices, backed by damages and fees, give Nevada residents assurance of transparent and accountable dealings throughout their lease term.

New Hampshire

(N.H. Rev. Stat. Ann. §358-P:1 et seq.)

New Hampshire's law has been recodified since earlier editions of this guide — it is now the **Rent-to-**

Own Agreement Act, and the lessor is specifically defined in the statute as a **"rent-to-own dealer."** The law requires prominent disclosures and reinstatement rights. Consumers may seek actual damages plus penalties, supporting Granite State families with accessible possession and a clearly defined right to acquire ownership, plus meaningful recourse if anything goes wrong.

New Jersey

New Jersey treats RTO agreements as **credit sales** under its Retail Installment Sales Act and broader consumer credit laws — there is no separate "rental-purchase," "lease-purchase," or "rent-to-own" agreement defined in New Jersey's operative consumer-protection statute. This classification requires clear cost disclosures and provides enhanced remedies typical of lending protections. New Jersey consumers often benefit from stronger safeguards against excessive markups and additional recourse through the state's robust consumer protection framework.

New Mexico

(N.M. Stat. Ann. §§57-26-1 to 57-26-13 — Rental-Purchase Agreement Act)

New Mexico requires full disclosure of the cash price, total payments necessary to acquire ownership, and reinstatement rights under its **Rental-Purchase Agreement** law, including a clearly disclosed early purchase option. Damages and attorney fees for violations give New Mexico consumers clear accountability and the confidence to use RTO responsibly.

New York

(N.Y. Pers. Prop. Law §§500 to 510)

New York's statute — recently recodified, and now found at a different section than in older references — governs the **Rental-Purchase Agreement**. It requires clear contracts and provides reinstatement opportunities, plus a statutory early purchase option with a required disclosure chart showing exactly what it would cost to acquire ownership after each payment. Remedies under general consumer protection statutes — including damages for deceptive practices — give New Yorkers robust tools for ensuring a fair RTO experience from start to finish.

North Carolina

(N.C. Gen. Stat. §25A-1 et seq. — Retail Installment Sales Act)

North Carolina does not have a dedicated rent-to-own statute, and it does not define a "rental-purchase agreement," "lease-purchase agreement," or "rent-to-own agreement" anywhere in its code. Instead, qualifying RTO transactions may fall under the Retail Installment Sales Act when they meet the definition of a consumer credit sale — for example, when total payments are substantially equivalent to the value of the goods and the consumer holds an "option to acquire ownership upon full compliance." The Act requires specific disclosures of costs and terms, regulates finance charges where applicable, and provides consumer protections against unconscionable practices, with remedies for violations. Because it treats certain RTO agreements more like financed purchases, consumers may receive enhanced cost transparency and stronger recourse options under this framework or North Carolina's Unfair and Deceptive Trade Practices Act. North Carolinians are encouraged to review their contract carefully to understand its classification, but the application of retail installment rules generally provides solid safeguards for gaining possession of household essentials without creating traditional long-term debt obligations.

North Dakota

(N.D. Cent. Code ch. 47-15.1)

North Dakota's law governs the **Consumer Rental Purchase Agreement** and requires disclosures of total costs to acquire ownership of the property, along with reinstatement rights. Remedies include damages and fees, giving North Dakota consumers confidence in a well-regulated RTO arrangement.

Ohio

(Ohio Rev. Code §§1351.01 to 1351.09)

Ohio's chapter on "Lease-Purchase Agreements" governs the **Lease-Purchase Agreement** and mandates point-of-sale tags and contract disclosures of the cash price and total payments needed to acquire ownership. In fact, one section of Ohio law is titled exactly that — "Acquiring Ownership When 50% of Payments Equals Cash Price" — meaning ownership can transfer automatically partway through your agreement. Generous reinstatement windows and remedies — including statutory damages and attorney fees — protect consumers throughout the arrangement. Ohioans benefit from transparent, flexible terms that keep every option open.

Oklahoma

(Okla. Stat. tit. 59, §§1950.1 to 1950.10 — Rental-Purchase Agreement Act)

Oklahoma's **Rental-Purchase Agreement** law emphasizes clear terms and reinstatement rights, and specifically requires that consumers be told they can obtain ownership through what the statute calls "ownership options" built into the agreement. Violations allow recovery of damages, supporting fair access to RTO for Oklahoma consumers and ensuring that merchants are held to their obligations.

Oregon

(Or. Rev. Stat. §§646A.120 to 646A.134)

Oregon governs the **Lease-Purchase Agreement** and requires detailed disclosures and reasonable reinstatement with clear limits on fees. Consumer remedies include damages and attorney fees, giving Oregon residents strong confidence in the transparency and accountability of the path to acquiring ownership.

Pennsylvania

(42 Pa. Cons. Stat. §6901 et seq. — Rental-Purchase Agreement Act)

Pennsylvania's **Rental-Purchase Agreement Act** requires clear and conspicuous disclosures covering all essential terms — including costs, payment schedules, and consumer rights. The law defines

RTO as an agreement for personal, family, or household use with an initial short term that renews automatically with each payment, distinctly separate from retail installment sales. You receive immediate possession and use of the merchandise, with the merchant retaining title until you complete all required payments or exercise a buyout option — Pennsylvania's specific statutory term for converting to ownership before your scheduled payments are complete. The statute works in tandem with Pennsylvania's Unfair Trade Practices and Consumer Protection Law to address deceptive or unfair practices. These disclosure requirements, combined with reinstatement rights and a fully regulated environment, ensure that RTO arrangements in Pennsylvania remain transparent and fair — giving Pennsylvanians flexible access to household goods without hidden terms or burdensome commitments.

Rhode Island

(R.I. Gen. Laws §§6-44-1 to 6-44-9 — Rhode Island Rental-Purchase Agreement Act)

Rhode Island's law mandates clear contracts and reinstatement options for what it calls a **Rental-Purchase Agreement**, with meaningful remedies for violations. The statute also guarantees an early purchase option: at any time after the initial payment, you may acquire ownership of the property simply by complying with the early purchase terms clearly set forth in your agreement. Rhode Islanders can approach RTO with confidence in its regulated, consumer-protective framework.

South Carolina

(S.C. Code Ann. §§37-2-701 to 37-2-713)

South Carolina's law, Part 7 of its Credit Sales chapter, defines and governs the **Consumer Rental-Purchase Agreement**. It requires clear disclosures and fair terms, with reinstatement rights and general consumer protections supporting responsible and confident use of RTO for immediate possession of household essentials and a clearly disclosed path to acquiring ownership.

South Dakota

(S.D. Codified Laws, Title 54, ch. 6A)

South Dakota's chapter, "Lease-Purchase Agreements for Personal Property," governs the **Lease-Purchase Agreement**. It focuses on transparency and reinstatement rights, with damages and fees for noncompliance giving consumers strong leverage to ensure fair treatment — and a clear, disclosed path to acquiring ownership — throughout their RTO arrangement.

Tennessee

(Tenn. Code Ann. §§47-18-601 to 47-18-614 – Tennessee Rental-Purchase Agreement Act)

Tennessee's law governs the **Rental-Purchase Agreement** and mandates detailed disclosures and reinstatement rights, with remedies tied to the state's consumer protection laws to ensure fair play and accountability for all parties as they work toward acquiring ownership of the property.

Texas

(Tex. Bus. & Com. Code §92.001 et seq. – Rental-Purchase Agreements)

Texas defines RTO as a short initial-period lease that renews automatically with each payment, with ownership available only after all required payments are completed under what the statute calls a **Rental-Purchase Agreement**. Merchants must use plain language in contracts and advertisements and must disclose whether an item is new or used, the cash price, payment amounts and timing, total payments needed to acquire ownership, any additional fees, and your reinstatement rights. You receive immediate possession while the merchant retains title. Reinstatement is available – generally by curing any default before the later of one week after the due date or half the regular payment period –

without losing credit for payments already made. The law prohibits certain unfair provisions and requires that any charges beyond periodic payments be reasonably related to the service provided. Texas's upfront transparency requirements and reinstatement protections give Texans a clear understanding of their lease terms and a fair opportunity to maintain possession even when a temporary payment delay occurs.

Utah

(Utah Code Ann. §§15-8-1 to 15-8-12 — Rental-Purchase Agreement Act)

Utah's **Rental-Purchase Agreement Act** provides clear disclosures, reinstatement rights, and remedies including damages and fees — establishing a straightforward and consumer-protective framework for both immediate possession and a clearly defined path to acquiring ownership throughout the state.

Vermont

(9 V.S.A. §41b — Rent-to-Own Agreements; Disclosure of Terms)

Vermont provides some of the most detailed consumer protections of any state, and its statute — like Connecticut's, New Hampshire's, and West Virginia's — calls the contract a **Rent-to-Own**

Agreement rather than a rental-purchase or lease-purchase agreement. Vermont also uses different party labels: the lessor is a "merchant" and you are a "consumer," not a "lessee." Full and conspicuous written disclosures of all key terms are required before you move forward, including the cash price (subject to statutory caps), the total payments needed to acquire ownership (capped at twice the maximum cash price in many cases), any additional fees, and your rights under the agreement. You must be given the opportunity to review the contract and even consult with a third party before committing. While you have possession, the merchant is responsible for maintaining the item in good working condition and handling repairs — with a replacement provided during service if needed. Reinstatement rights typically extend within five business days for monthly payments or three business days for more frequent schedules, by paying past-due amounts plus reasonable costs. After voluntarily returning an item, you may reinstate for up to 180 days. Vermont's law also guarantees a statutory option to purchase: at any time, you may acquire ownership by paying the cash price minus 50% of payments already made. Abusive collection or repossession practices are prohibited, and violations are treated as unfair and deceptive acts under Vermont's Consumer Protection Act. Vermont's strong disclosure rules, merchant maintenance responsibility, price-related caps, and generous reinstatement periods give

Vermonters exceptional confidence when choosing RTO for immediate possession of needed goods.

Virginia

(Va. Code Ann. §§59.1-207.17 to 59.1-207.27 — Virginia Lease-Purchase Agreement Act)

Virginia's law governs the **Lease-Purchase Agreement** and requires clear disclosures and reinstatement rights, with remedies supporting consumer confidence throughout the lease arrangement. Virginia's framework ensures that RTO consumers understand their rights — including the disclosed path to acquiring ownership — and have meaningful recourse available.

Washington

(Wash. Rev. Code §§63.19.010 to 63.19.100 — Washington Lease-Purchase Agreement Act)

Washington's law governs the **Lease-Purchase Agreement** and emphasizes full disclosures of total costs to acquire ownership, and provides flexible reinstatement rights, backed by consumer remedies. Washington State's framework gives residents confidence in the transparency and accountability of every RTO arrangement.

West Virginia

(W. Va. Code §§46B-1-101 to 46B-8-802)

West Virginia's chapter — titled "Regulation of the Rental of Consumer Goods Under Rent-to-Own Agreements" — governs the **Rent-to-Own Agreement**, with the lessor specifically defined in the statute as a "dealer." It provides detailed consumer protections, including required disclosures, reinstatement rights, and meaningful remedies for violations, plus a defined "rent-to-own charge" representing the total cost above retail value needed to acquire ownership — creating a well-rounded framework for safe and confident use of RTO across the state.

Wisconsin

Wisconsin treats RTO as a **credit sale** under its consumer lending laws (the Wisconsin Consumer Act), requiring enhanced disclosures and providing protections comparable to installment sales regulations. There is no separate "rental-purchase," "lease-purchase," or "rent-to-own" agreement defined in Wisconsin's operative statute — instead, the consumer becomes the owner of the property "upon full compliance with the terms of the agreement." This approach gives Wisconsin consumers strong tools against unfair terms and additional recourse through the state's consumer lending framework.

Wyoming

(Wyo. Stat. Ann. §§40-19-101 to 40-19-115 — Consumer Rental Purchase Agreement Act)

Wyoming requires clear contracts, reinstatement rights, and remedies including damages and attorney fees for its **Rental-Purchase Agreement** — supporting safe, informed, and confident use of RTO, with a clear path to acquiring ownership, throughout the state.

District of Columbia

(D.C. Code §§42-3671.01 to 42-3671.10 — Chapter 36B, Lease-Purchase Agreements)

The District of Columbia's law mandates consumer rights disclosures, fair-term requirements, reinstatement opportunities, and aligned consumer protections for what it calls a **Lease-Purchase Agreement**. D.C. residents can access household essentials through RTO with full transparency, a clearly disclosed path to acquiring ownership, and meaningful recourse if issues arise.

PLEASE NOTE

The information in this reference is provided for general consumer education and reflects statutes current at the time of publication. Laws are subject to change.

For the most current information in your state, contact your state's consumer protection office or visit the *Association of Professional Rental Organizations* website at rtohq.org. Statute citations sourced from APRO and verified against *The Rent-To-Own Revolution: A Definitive History of Advocacy and Consumer Access* (Smitherman & Krass, 2026).

* * *

Sources & References

Primary Sources

Association of Professional Rental Organizations (APRO). 2026. *50-State Model Lease Agreement Library*. Developed in partnership with Hudson Cook, LLP. rtohq.org

Baden, D., et al. 2020. "Access Over Ownership: Case Studies of Libraries of Things." *Sustainability* 12 (17): 7180.

Baxter, Robbie Kellman. 2015. *The Membership Economy: Find Your Super Users, Master the Forever Transaction, and Build Recurring Revenue*. New York: McGraw-Hill.

Cobzaru, Paula, and Alexandru Tugui. 2024. "The Subscription Economy and Its Contribution to the Global Economy." *Journal of Economics and Development Studies* 12 (2): 45–58.

Godin, Seth. 1999. *Permission Marketing: Turning Strangers into Friends, and Friends into Customers*. New York: Simon & Schuster.

Godin, Seth. 2003. *Purple Cow: Transform Your Business by Being Remarkable*. New York: Portfolio/Penguin.

Godin, Seth. 2007. *The Dip: A Little Book That Teaches You When to Quit (and When to Stick)*. New York: Portfolio/Penguin.

Mordor Intelligence. 2025. *U.S. Self-Storage Market – Industry Analysis, Size, Share, Growth Trends, and Forecast* (2025–2030).

Recurly. 2026. *The 2026 State of Subscriptions*. Recurly Subscription Intelligence Report.

Smitherman, Charles, and Ryan Krass. 2026. *The Rent-to-Own Revolution: The Definitive Industry History of Advocacy and Consumer Access*. APRO.

United For ALICE. n.d. ALICE (Asset Limited, Income Constrained, Employed) *Research Framework*. unitedforalice.org

Velma, R. 2025. "Subscription Economy and the Transformation of Ownership: A Review of Value Perceptions and Retention Strategies." *Advances in Consumer Research*.

Yardi Matrix. 2025–2026. *Self-Storage Market Reports*.

Zuora. 2025. *Subscription Economy Index 2025*. Zuora Inc.

* * *

Government & Economic Sources

Government & Regulatory

Congressional Research Service. 2021. *Overview of Rural Credit Markets*.

Consumer Financial Protection Bureau (CFPB). 2022–2023. *Reports on Rural Banking Deserts*. Documents that rural communities are ten times more likely than urban communities to be banking deserts, with over 2,100 banking deserts identified nationwide.

Consumer Financial Protection Bureau (CFPB). 2025. *Consumer Credit Card Market Report*. Source for: $160 billion in credit card interest paid in 2024; average APR of 25.2% for general-purpose cards and 31.3% for store cards; 15–20% of cardholders making only minimum payments.

Federal Reserve Board. 2024–2025. *Survey of Household Economics and Decisionmaking* (SHED), part of the broader Report on the Economic Well-Being of U.S. Households.

Federal Reserve & National Community Reinvestment Coalition (NCRC). n.d. Banking desert concentration data. Documents the geographic distribution of banking deserts, with the majority in rural America.

Federal Trade Commission (FTC). 2000. *Survey of Rent-to-Own Customers*. Bureau of Economics Staff Report. Key finding: 68% of RTO customers lived in non-suburban areas.

Economic & Market Data

Association of Professional Rental Organizations (APRO). *2025. Rent-to-Own Industry Health Survey.* Available at: rtohq.org/rent-to-own-industry-statistics

National Association of Realtors and U.S. Census Bureau. Various years. Housing affordability data. Median home price was 2.5× median household income in 1970, rising to 8–12× in coastal markets in recent years.

* * *

A Note on the Access Ecosystem

The companies, platforms, and services mentioned in this book are provided as starting points for readers who wish to explore the access mindset in their own lives. They represent a rapidly evolving landscape — readers are encouraged to verify current offerings, terms, and availability directly with each provider. Any mention of a company in this book is not intended to be an endorsement, but a starting place on your exploration.

See the **Transparency Note from the Author**

* * *

Where to Find More Access

Where to Find More Access — Brief Starter List

As stated in Chapter 2, the rent-to-own industry alone generates $11.5 billion in annual U.S. revenue. It serves 4.6 million American households each year, roughly one in every 29 households, with nearly 3 million active customers at any given moment. The industry supports over 42,000 American jobs and invests nearly $2 billion annually in new inventory to keep essential goods flowing to the people who need them most.

According to APRO's most recent industry survey, there are 5,798 rent-to-own brick-and-mortar stores across the United States and that number is growing. There is very likely an RTO store within a reasonable distance of where you live right now.

But the RTO stores are only the beginning. Tens of thousands of familiar retailers across the country offer lease-to-own options at the point of purchase. Most shoppers walk past these options every week without realizing they exist.

This list is only a brief starting point. It does not begin to capture the full landscape of access options available to today's consumer. Remember, stores change and rename, so do searches locally to find more access near you.

* * *

The Top RTO Nationwide Chains

- **Rent-A-Center** — Originally *ColorTyme* (mentioned in Chapter 1), holds the #1 spot and is in all 50 states, plus Puerto Rico and DC. They offer furniture, appliances, electronics and computers.
- **Aaron's** — Second ranked, offering furniture, appliances, and electronics, with retail stores in 47 states and Canada, plus an e-commerce platform.
- **RNR Tire Express** — The nation's third largest and its fastest-growing, having expanded by nearly 40% in recent years into 31 states and Canada. RNR focuses exclusively on tires, wheels and automotive with an "Everyone's Approved" philosophy and a Customer Care Package that sets the standard for the category.
- **Buddy's Home Furnishings** — In relative tie for the #3 spot, offers furniture, appliances, and electronics across 18 states and Guam.
- **Bestway Rent-to-Own** — A regional chain serving local communities across ten states, offers home goods as well.

Beyond these national names, America is rich with regional chains and independent owner-operators — family businesses that have been steadily serving their neighbors for decades. Many of these local stores are the only financial lifeline in their communities. There are simply too many to list, but they are out there, on main streets and in strip malls, in small towns and rural communities across the country. You may just find one closer than you think.

* * *

Retailers You May Recognize Offering Lease-to-Own

(Ask at the stores — you may be surprised)

- **Electronics & Technology** — Best Buy · GameStop · Walmart · Amazon (*select sellers*)
- **Computers, Tablets & Gaming** — Best Buy · Dell · HP · GameStop · Aaron's · Rent-A-Center (*MacBooks, iPads, Samsung, LG, Sony and more — often with no-credit-needed access and flexible weekly or bi-weekly payments*)
- **Furniture & Home** — Ashley HomeStore · Rooms to Go · Conn's HomePlus · Big Lots · P.C. Richards & Son · Wayfair
- **Home Improvement** — Home Depot (*refrigerators, washers, dryers, ranges, dishwashers, power tools, air compressors, generators, patio sets, and outdoor living items*) · Lowe's (*appliances, lighting, ceiling fans, patio furniture, grills, and seasonal outdoor items — Lowe's publishes a specific Leasable Items List available in-store and online*)
- **Mattresses** — Mattress Firm
- **Jewelry** — Kay Jewelers · Zales · Reeds Jewelers (*including engagement rings — ask for the lease option*)

- **Sporting Goods & Outdoors** — Bass Pro Shops · Dick's Sporting Goods
- **Musical Instruments** — Guitar Center · local music shops (*the original access model*)
- **Tools, Lawn & Garden Equipment** — Aaron's · Rent-A-Center · Home Depot · Lowe's (*riding mowers, zero-turn mowers, push mowers, power tools, generators — many with maintenance included and no credit needed*)
- **Storage Buildings & Sheds** — Leonard · Cook Portable Warehouses · Tuff Shed · Fisher Barns (*and thousands of regional dealers nationwide*)

* * *

The Hybrid Access Programs

(Access philosophy, different name)

These programs were available at the time of my research for this book and availability could always change, so do your own due-diligence when shopping for your personal needs.

- **Apple iPhone Upgrade Program** — After 12 payments, you can upgrade to a new iPhone and trade in your current one, with AppleCare+ included throughout. Apple does not openly label it lease-to-own, but the elements are unmistakably familiar — periodic payments, upgrade at a milestone, trade-in required. Millions of Americans participate without thinking of it in those terms.
- **T-Mobile Go5G Next · AT&T Next Up · Verizon Device Payment** — The major carriers all offer device upgrade programs that function as revolving lease cycles, often bundled with service plans. Pay a portion of the device cost, trade in for credit toward a new one, repeat. A hybrid of lease, subscription, and upgrade — and one of the most widely used access arrangements in America.

- **Cricket Wireless · Boost Mobile · Straight Talk** — Prepaid carrier brands offer similar trade-in and upgrade programs, often with lower entry requirements and more flexible terms.

A Final Note

When in doubt, ask. At any retailer, for any product, the question *"Do you offer a lease or payment access option?"* costs nothing and may open a door you didn't know was there.

For the most current industry information and to find APRO-member stores near you, visit APRO at rtohq.org.

* * *

About the Author

Marian Snow writes about the real financial decisions people make when life refuses to follow a perfect plan.

That perspective wasn't learned in a classroom. It came from many decades of working inside financial systems.

As CFO of a multi-million-dollar mortgage banking firm for 17 years, Marian saw firsthand how lending, credit, and money genuinely work in practice. At the same time, through her work in real estate, she sat across the table from hard-working families navigating those same systems.

Infinite Upgrades grew from those insights.

Her first book, *Stop Sitting on Your Assets*, reached the #1 spot on Amazon in both Real Estate and Retirement Planning.

Infinite Upgrades is her second title, and the one a lifetime of real-world experience made inevitable.

Made in United States
Cleveland, OH
06 November 2026

47762625R00161